WHEN GOOD MEN ARE TEMPTED

WHEN GOOD MEN ARE TEMPTED

BILL PERKINS

ZondervanPublishingHouse
Grand Rapids, Michigan

A Division of HarperCollins*Publishers*

When Good Men Are Tempted
Copyright © 1997 by Bill Perkins

Requests for information should be addressed to:

ZondervanPublishingHouse
Grand Rapids, Michigan 49530

Library of Congress Cataloging-in-Publication Data

Perkins, Bill, 1949–
     When good men are tempted / Bill Perkins.
          p.   cm.
     ISBN: 0-310-21566-8 (sofcover)
     1. Husbands—Sexual behavior.   2. Husbands—Religious life.   3. Lust—
Religious aspects—Christianity.   4. Sex—Religious aspects—Christianity.   5. Sex in
marriage.   Sex instruction for men.   I. Title.
HQ28.P47   1997
305.31—dc21   97–34175
                                                                                                  CIP

Published in association with the literary agency of Wolgemuth and Associates, Inc.

Interior design by Jody DeNeef

Printed in the United States of America

---

04 05 /❖DC/ 31 30 29 28 27 26 25 24

Contents

PART ONE

Understanding
the Struggle

Chapter One

Why Naked Women Look So Good

This chapter was birthed one Friday night while I was turning on my sprinkler system. As I walked across my yard, I noticed that my neighbors' lights were on. Curious as to why the neighbors were up so late, I approached the fence and looked through the slats. I expected to see a handful of people playing cards inside their home. Instead I saw a beautiful young woman talking on the phone. That wouldn't have been any big deal if she had been dressed. But she wasn't.

Instantly my eyes locked on her. Adrenaline rushed through my body. After gazing at her for a few seconds, I pried myself away from the fence. As I walked away, I wondered why a naked woman was so beautiful. And why would her beauty affect me that way?

Since that experience fifteen years ago, I've addressed thousands of men and talked personally with others. I've administered confidential surveys to find out what men are really thinking and doing. In the process, I've discovered that every man has his own personal battle with lust. Nobody escapes its appeal. Nobody.

If you're like a lot of guys I know, you want to win that battle. You want to enjoy a woman's beauty without compromising your character. Yet you're probably finding that purity isn't easy to maintain. Especially nowadays! Sensuality winks at you from the television set and lures you from a computer monitor. It calls you from magazines and entices you at work. Walking away from sinful indulgence in the appeal of women isn't easy. But we can do it. I'm convinced that taking the first step begins with understanding why naked women look so good.

The Mystery of a Woman's Beauty

When I saw my wife's body for the first time, I felt I was beholding something almost holy. Nothing in all of creation compared with the beauty of her nakedness.

Evolutionists strip the mystery from a woman's beauty. They tell us men are attracted to naked women because of natural selection. They reason that if men didn't find women attractive, they wouldn't be inclined to reproduce. Of course, this reduces sexual magnetism to a purely biological, animalistic experience. It isn't. God created men with sexual appetites. He wired us in such a way that we're attracted to women.

There's more here than some sort of accidental evolutionary programming. The book of Proverbs addresses the feelings between a man and a woman. Agur son of Jekah described four things too amazing for him to grasp. One of them was the way of a man with a woman (Prov. 30:19). There's something mysterious that occurs between a man and a woman. It can't be fully understood, because it's a mystery.

That answer probably disappoints you. It shouldn't. God has created something wonderful for men, something that defies understanding. If we could figure it out, there would be no mystery. Regardless of how old a man gets, the appeal of a woman is still there. As we age we can even heighten this appeal by creating in our imagination what eludes our experience. This mystery outlives us all. And the mystery isn't evil. It's good. It's a wonderful gift from God.

While the essence of this mystery is beyond human understanding, there are some aspects of it that are quite simple. For instance, naked women are beautiful because we seldom see them that way. This whole idea of nakedness is a special treat God has given only to people. Animals, for instance, can't be naked.

The Hidden Treasure

Over the years we've had several dogs. Our most recent was a 185-pound Great Dane appropriately named Big. I'd take him for walks and people would ask, "What's his name?"

"Big," I'd say.

"Yeah, he really is big. But what's his name?" they'd ask.

"His name is Big," I'd tell them.

It's amazing how quickly I bonded with that big guy. If you have a dog, you understand how fast they become a member of the family. They ride in our cars with us. They sleep with us (forget that one with Big). We talk to them as though they could understand us. Occasionally my boys even dressed Big in clothes. They'd slip red Nike shorts over his hind legs, and a white sweatshirt over his front legs. Next they'd secure a hat to his head and sunglasses on his nose.

While Big looked cute all dressed up, the truth is that he didn't need shorts and a sweatshirt. Why? Because even without them he wasn't naked. No animal is ever regarded as naked. Think about it for a minute. Have you ever seen a dog strolling down the street without shorts and a shirt and wondered why it wasn't dressed? Of course not! And no animal has ever been issued a ticket for indecent exposure.

Nothing can be naked in the same sense people are naked. Not trees, rocks, dogs, or dolphins. As men, we're not curious about the nakedness of an animal or plant. How could we be? They can't be naked.

Women can be. Yet they seldom are. The women we see every day at work and in our communities are all clothed. A naked woman reveals what is almost always hidden from male eyes—the beauty of her body.

Comedian and television personality Tim Allen said he'll never forget the first time he saw a picture of a naked woman. He said, "In a way, the picture was both frightening and reassuring. I realized for the first time that, dumb as it sounds, *all women are naked under their clothes....* That discovery made me distrust all women forever: they're hiding this! They have this power and I didn't even know it. It's just under their clothes!"[1]

Allen raises an issue that most men can identify with. Namely, how can women walk around every day and hide something so wonderful? And how can they pretend they don't know what they're doing?

I find his comments amusing and helpful. Amusing because they so openly express what many men feel but would never say—at least, they wouldn't put it in writing. Helpful because they reveal part of the reason why naked women look so good: men want to see something beautiful that's been hidden from them.

The opening pages of the Bible give us additional insight into the mystery of a woman's appeal.

Beholding a Masterpiece

I sometimes imagine what it must have been like for Adam the first time he saw Eve. He could honestly tell her, "You're the most beautiful woman I've ever seen!"

Actually, the creation of Eve resulted from a problem Adam had—a problem he wasn't even aware of. After each creative day, God looked at what he had made and announced that it was "good." Following the sixth and final day, during which he made Adam, God declared that his work was "very good" (Gen. 1:31).

But when God saw that Adam was alone, he said it was "not good" (Gen. 2:18). The Lord then determined to make a helper suitable for, or corresponding to, Adam—a helper who would complete him.

Before God did this, Adam needed to realize his need. To accomplish that, God had him name all the animals. Nobody knows how long it took, but I'd guess Adam must have spent months or years naming all the creatures that paraded before him. Adam must have noticed that the animals came in pairs, males and females. And he must have noticed that there was no creature who corresponded to him.

When Adam's sense of aloneness reached a sufficient level of intensity, God stepped in. He caused Adam to fall into a deep sleep and performed the first act of surgery. He took a rib from Adam's side and custom-made a companion for him. The first man was made from the earth; the first woman was made from the man.

Everything about her was designed and shaped by God so she and Adam would perfectly complement each other. The Master Artist who sculpted the universe spared nothing in the creation of this masterpiece.

I've asked men on numerous occasions what they think is the most beautiful sight on earth. Given a choice between a blazing desert sunset, a shimmering sunrise, an ocean wave crashing against a rock, a blossoming flower, or a gorgeous woman, they'll always say, "A gorgeous woman."

God knew what he was doing when he made the first woman. He made sure her eyes, lips, hair, breasts, legs, feet, arms, and hands would be just what Adam wanted and needed. She would empty his world of aloneness—an aloneness that even God couldn't meet (now, that's a profound thought).

Until Adam's rib was shaped into the form of Eve, creation was incomplete. It existed in a "not good" state.

When God had put the final touch on his masterpiece, he unveiled her. Adam awakened in the recovery room, rubbed his eyes, and climbed to his feet. As he wandered through the garden, Adam didn't have a clue as to what awaited him. Not a clue.

Suddenly she was there in front of him. Adam had never seen a woman, and the one he beheld was a ten in every possible way: physically, spiritually, emotionally, psychologically, intellectually. She was everything he needed in another person. And she was unstained by a broken past and wounded conscience. Eve was truly innocent.

Not only was Eve perfect for Adam, he was perfect for her. He possessed everything she needed in the one who would correspond to her.

The text tells us that when Adam saw her, he said, "She shall be called 'woman'" (Gen. 2:23). Whenever I describe this meeting while officiating at a wedding ceremony, I mention that the Hebrew word for "man" is "Ish," and the word for "woman" is "Isha." I suggest that Adam may have beheld Eve and said, "Ish" and then added an expression of wonder and pleasure: "aaaaaaaaaaaaaaaaaaaaaaaaa." That may not have been what happened, but it makes sense to me. If Adam had spoken English, he might have said, "Wo! Man!"

No wonder naked women look so good—they're God's masterpiece. But they're something else, too. *Women fill up what's lacking in men.*

The Completer

With the creation of Eve, Adam lost a rib. With the appearance of Eve, Adam discovered the one who would make him complete. Without her Adam was like a pen without ink, or a ship without a sail—he was incomplete. Part of him was literally missing. When Adam met Eve, he came face to face with the part of himself that was absent.

While the Bible doesn't say this, I wonder if the beauty of a woman's body is somehow linked to a man's search for completeness. At the deepest level of a man's subconscious, is there a part of him that craves finding the one who will make him whole? Are men searching for the part that was taken from them? Are they seeking the one without whom they'll forever feel incomplete?

I don't mean to imply that single people can't find fulfillment. After all, Jesus was single and his life was certainly full. But single people have learned to live with what is usually a mild case of aloneness, a sense that they are by themselves, that they are lacking something or someone—something or someone they've learned to live without.

I think that for men, that sense of aloneness or lacking is a figurative need to find their missing rib, a need to discover the person who will make them complete. I suspect that one reason naked women look so good is because they have a unique power to make a man whole. In the moment a man gazes at a woman's naked beauty, he experiences, for a fleeting second, the hope of being complete. When he is physically joined to her, he feels complete.

The Glow of Nakedness

In his book *The Mystery of Marriage,* Mike Mason notes that the human body "possesses a glory that is unique in all the earth."[2] By glory he meant "awe-inspiring beauty." In a sense, our bodies reveal who we are. They're the physical expression of our soul and spirit. The body of a woman is more than skin and bones and blood and hair. It is the veil of her person.

Several times in the Old Testament, we find God revealing himself with a physical manifestation. He did that when he first appeared to Moses on the mountain as a fire in a bush. Later he appeared to Moses and the Israelites at Mount Sinai as a dense cloud filled with lightning. The glory of God was so great at Mount Sinai that the face of Moses would literally glow after being in the presence of God's glory.

Theologians refer to these manifestations of God as his "shining glory." They reveal the power and beauty of God. In a sense, I think our physical bodies have their own shining glory. It's a beauty that in some small way reveals us as the masterpiece of God's creation.[3] As men, we never tire of looking at a woman's beauty. It's as if we want to view it from every angle and, like Moses on the mountain, enter her glory.

A Search for Intimacy

Nakedness assumes intimacy. It assumes that the person who has disrobed in your presence trusts you. They're willing to let you see their beauty and their imperfections. We do that with people we believe will love and accept us—warts and all.

Adam and Eve had such intimacy. After God brought them together, "The man and his wife were both naked, and they felt no shame" (Gen. 2:25). Their physical nakedness portrayed the nakedness that existed at a deeper level—a spiritual and emotional level. Adam and Eve were intimate in every sense of the word.

While men shy away from intimacy, they still need it. The problem is, we've been programmed to believe we must be self-sufficient. Real men, we've been told, are independent and rugged. Annual polls continually tell us John Wayne is one of the most popular actors of all time. Men love his rugged individualism. And while he's stood the test of time, every year Hollywood parades a new set of ideal men across the silver screen. Nobody illustrates this ideal better than James Bond.

He can accomplish superhuman feats without anybody's help, without ever sharing his inner self with anybody.

While men grit their teeth and try to go it alone, something inside cries for an intimate connection at the deepest level. I believe that naked women are beautiful because their nakedness tells a man, "I'm here for you. I'm yours. I've bared myself for your eyes." That unspoken—or spoken—statement tells a man he's safe. It tells him he's loved. It tells him someone wants to be intimate with him.

Because nakedness presupposes intimacy, seeing a naked woman provides men with an intimate connection—even if it's a superficial one. However, true intimacy can only occur in a safe setting, in an environment of love and trust.

Enjoying a Woman's Nakedness

It surprises some people to hear that God celebrates sex. He not only created men so they find pleasure in playing with a naked woman, he created the ideal playground: marriage. It's in that setting that there is security and commitment. People who exchange marriage vows are making a commitment to pursue the intimacy that nakedness presupposes. Within marriage men can fully celebrate the beauty of a woman's body.

Solomon certainly did. And he wasn't reluctant to express his pleasure. Tucked away in the middle of the Old Testament is the poetic book Song of Songs. The book describes the love between Solomon and his bride. The language is so sexually charged that for years theologians preferred to interpret the book allegorically rather than literally. By allowing Solomon to represent Christ, and his young bride the church, they could get around the sexual language. But such an interpretation doesn't do justice to the text or to God's high view of sexual intimacy.

Eyes That Excite

The most explicit language is found in chapter 4, where Solomon describes the first evening of their honeymoon. Once the two are alone, the king tells his lover that the look of her eyes is enough to excite him (v. 9). The Jewish people possessed a land that was often described as the land of "milk and honey." It was a land of great richness and offered pleasure to those who occupied it. Similarly, the one Solomon held in his arms provided him with both pleasure and well-being (v. 11).

A Garden That Pleases

In his book *A Song for Lovers,* my friend S. Craig Glickman said of the couple, "Their love is consummated in one of the shyest and most delicate of love scenes in world literature."[4] There's nothing crude or rash in Solomon's speech. Instead he compares his bride to a garden and fountain (vv. 12–15). He makes a gentle reference to her virginity by noting that the fountain is sealed and the garden locked (v. 12). Nobody else has entered her garden. Finally the night for a visitor has arrived. Solomon delights in the aroma and taste of her love.

In response to his expressions of delight, she invites him to come into her garden (v. 16). Before doing so, he finds himself swept away by her beauty and describes it more fully. Her garden is like a paradise of fruits, flowers, blossoms, trees, and aromatic spices.[5] As most men would attest, that most private of all places has become for Solomon a place of greatest pleasure.

Is she ready for his love? Indeed. Solomon declared that her fountain has become a "well of flowing water" (v. 15). Sexually aroused, she pleads with him to "come into his garden and taste its choice fruits" (v. 16).

A Word of Approval

After allowing us to peek into his honeymoon suite, Solomon permits us to hear the final words that were uttered that night. Amazingly, they weren't spoken by Solomon or his bride. They were spoken by God. And how did the creator of a woman's beauty respond to the pleasure the couple enjoyed? He said, "Eat, O friends, and drink; drink your fill, O lovers" (Song 5:1).

The One who created them man and woman gave hearty approval to all they had done. He delighted in their finding pleasure in each other's arms.

The Bridle

God intended the act of sexual intimacy to be among the most powerful and pleasurable experiences of life. In the joining together of a man and woman, the two become "one flesh." Their bodies are literally linked together. During those exhilarating moments, the man and the one created from him are whole again. They are one.

God's ideal is for this oneness to take place within the safety of marriage. Why? In part because marriage enables a man to control the savage beast within, the creature whose appetites for sensual pleasure constantly test a man's resolve. That creature never gives up wanting to run wild.

I remember growing up in Roswell, New Mexico. Outside of town my family owned some land where we trained horses. Early on, my dad acquainted me with a saddle and bridle. While the saddle helps a rider stay on a horse, it's the bridle that brings the horse under control.

Without the bridle of marriage, our passions will run out of control—hurting us and others. Our sexual appetites are powerful. They must be trained and controlled.

A Broken Bridle

Of course, if our marriages are going to become the playground in which we enjoy a woman's nakedness, we must be attracted to our wife. Yesterday a man told me he no longer found his wife appealing. He informed her that the only hope he saw for their marriage was for her to get a "boob job." She no longer "turned him on," and he figured that the only solution was for her to improve her physical appearance.

His thinking is based on the idea that sexual attraction is exclusively linked to a tight body, youth, or the physical appearance deemed beautiful by our society. If he's right, the key to a dynamic sex life is an endless series of face-lifts, tummy-tucks, breast implants, and liposuction procedures.

But his reasoning is flawed. The magnetism of a magnet is based not on the physical appearance of the magnet but on the makeup of the magnet. It's what's on the inside that pulls the opposite poles together.

When a man and woman are no longer physically attracted to one another, it indicates that their relationship with God and with each other is broken. Something on the inside is distorted.

Once a man turns his back on God, his wedding vows have little value. In a very real sense, he's taken the bridle off and dropped it to the ground. He has made up his mind to meet his sexual needs in the manner he thinks will work best.

Instead of harnessing his passions and directing them toward his wife, he's allowing them to run wild. When that happens, he no longer treats his wife as unique, as the one who completes him, as the one whose body carries its own beautiful glory, as a person. In that setting, a man sees his wife as an obstacle to his own sensual gratification, as someone he must change to meet his needs, or get away from so his needs can be met by another woman.

Such thinking is the opposite of what God has created men to do. He has commanded us to focus our sexual energies on satisfying our wife—not ourselves. Men are to always remember that their own body is there for their wife (1 Cor. 7:3–5). Because of how God made men, it's as a man gives his wife pleasure with his words and caresses that he experiences her beauty. It's as a man focuses on meeting his wife's needs that he finds the greatest sexual pleasure (we'll talk about this more in chapter 12).

That's the ideal we must strive for, because anything else is an illusion and not reality. It's the lofty goal I want to work toward in this book so we can act consistently with how we're made. Then, and only then, will we experience the kind of intimacy and pleasure God intends us to find in the arms of our wife.

What About Other Women?

Of course, there is a problem that stands in the way. Even in the best of times, you'll find other women beautiful. Their appeal may be so strong that it pulls you away from your wife. Indeed, the beauty of your wife's nakedness may be eclipsed by that of other women.

This reality is the issue I'll discuss in the next chapter. There you'll find out why women you can't have—or shouldn't have—often look better than the one God has given you.

Thinking It Through

1. Can you remember the first time you saw a naked woman, either in person or in a photograph? How did it affect you?

2. How do you think most men believe God feels about the sexual attraction men have for women? Why do you think they view God that way?

3. How does God view the sexual pleasure a man finds in his wife? What does Song of Songs 5:1 tell us about this question?

4. Why do men find women so attractive?

As you think through these questions, ask God to help you view women and sex as he does.

Chapter Two

Why Other Women Look Better

"What took so long?" my wife asked.

I squirmed as I thought about how I'd answer her question.

Normally I'd run outside, turn on the sprinkler system, and be back inside in less than a minute. But as I mentioned in the last chapter, on that particular Friday night I got sidetracked by something I saw through a neighbor's window.

"I wasn't gone that long," I answered defensively.

"Bill, what took you so long?" she persisted.

"I saw a naked woman," I whispered. I figured that if I answered her softly, she might not hear me.

"What do you mean, you saw a naked woman?" she asked in a loud voice—much louder than mine had been.

"You know," I said. "I saw a naked woman while I was standing at the fence looking through our neighbor's window."

"What were you doing looking through our neighbor's window in the middle of the night?"

I explained that my voyeurism wasn't premeditated. "I saw the light on in their house and wondered what they were doing," I said.

I liked seeing that woman. In fact, before I drifted off to sleep I realized I liked it a lot. I liked it so much it scared me, because I knew I'd be tempted to look again. And the last thing I wanted to do was tell the guys in my small group.

Every Saturday morning I would get together with three other men. We met to encourage and challenge each other as husbands, fathers, and followers of Christ. These guys were the spiritual leaders of the church. They were the men others looked to as role models. The last thing I wanted to do was admit to *them* what I had done. But I knew that the best way to deal with temptation is to get it out in the open. I decided that telling them was the best chance I had of cutting off this problem before it got out of control.

That decision led to a bigger surprise than the one I received while gazing through my neighbor's window. At our next meeting, the three men looked at each other nervously after I shared my story with them. One of them shifted in his chair, cleared his throat, and said, "I know how you feel. I've been watching my neighbors for almost two years! From the second floor of our house, I can look right into their bedroom."

No sooner had he finished talking than a second man said, "I've been watching my neighbor for a year. She's a single woman in her mid-twenties and cleans her house in the nude. Because our houses are close together, I have a clear view of her at night."

Both of these men said they had repeatedly promised themselves they would never look again, but they couldn't resist the temptation. I wondered if the same thing would happen to me. Not wanting to take any chances, I did something to make sure it wouldn't happen again. And my friends followed my lead. In chapter 11 I'll tell you what we did to protect ourselves and our neighbors' privacy.

As I left that meeting, I realized in a fresh way that there's a dangerous side to the magnetic appeal of a woman's body, a side that has the power to enslave a man, the power to make him do things that violate everything he believes to be right and good, the power to destroy him and those he loves.

The Dark Side

You've probably noticed that often the most attractive women are those you can't or shouldn't have. If so, you realize something about yourself that's true of all men. Namely, we're all fascinated by things that are off-limits. I know I am. Early in my life, I noticed that often the things I *shouldn't* do looked better to me than the things I *should* do.

I remember being told not to eat candy before dinner. But candy always tasted better than dinner. And hot dogs always tasted better than broccoli.

Once I found a copy of *Playboy* magazine. I was fascinated by the pictures. My parents told me I wasn't supposed to look at pictures of naked women. But I thought the undressed women I saw in *Playboy* looked better than fully dressed women.

When I started driving, the law told me to drive within the posted speed limit always. But going fast was more fun than going slow.

I wish I could say everything has turned around for me as an adult. A while back my doctor told me my cholesterol is in the high-risk range. As I left his office, he handed me a list of foods I'm not supposed to eat. Did the list give me permission to eat ice cream and chocolate cake? No way! Most of the foods I love to eat are off-limits. And my doctor's recommended diet tastes like Styrofoam and water.

As an avid sports fan, I enjoy reading *Sports Illustrated*. When the annual swimsuit edition comes out, I don't look at the cover and say, "What a dog." As beautiful as my wife is, I still find other women appealing. In fact, they're often *more* appealing to me than Cindy.

The first time I shared this secret with my wife, she was hurt, although deep down I think she already knew. Cindy feared she had lost her appeal—as though my being attracted to other women was somehow her fault.

"It's not just me!" I assured her. "All men are that way. Look at the rich and famous men who marry a Hollywood star only to tire of her beauty in a few years, toss her aside, and then marry another, younger one." I told Cindy that my being attracted to other women didn't mean I wasn't capable of having her be the most appealing woman to me. But keeping her in the number one spot would require both understanding and discipline: understanding of myself and why other women often look better to me, and discipline to make choices that will focus my sexual energies on my wife.

Forbidden Fruit

My search for understanding drove me to reformulate the question from "Why do naked women look so good?" to "Why do *other* naked women sometimes look better?"

In the last chapter, we saw that God wired men in such a way that we delight in a woman's beauty. That's good! It's healthy and normal. But that appeal becomes harmful when our appreciation for a woman's beauty turns into lust, when we no longer see her as a person but as a body to be used purely for our pleasure. The transition from admiration to lust follows a well-worn path, one that was first visited by Adam and Eve. While the issue they faced didn't have to do with sexual lust, the trap they stepped into is the same.

Whenever I read the account of their experience in the garden, I can't help but shake my head in amazement. I'd like to think that if I had everything they possessed, I'd be immune to temptation. But of course I wouldn't be. And neither would you.

Something happened to those two that sheds considerable light on our struggle. To begin with, there was nothing inherently wrong with the fruit they were told not to eat (Gen. 2:17). The fruit wasn't poisonous. It wasn't rotten. It was something good that God told Adam and Eve to avoid. Why? To test their willingness to serve him, and to give them an opportunity to exercise their free will. They didn't have to obey. God gave them the freedom to choose what they would do with their lives.

Sometimes wrong things are good things that are off-limits. On other occasions wrong things are good things used to excess. Certainly there's nothing wrong with sex or the beauty of a naked woman. God made us sexual creatures, and he approves of the pleasure we derive from sexual intimacy. But sex becomes wrong and harmful when it's enjoyed in a way forbidden by God.

That's not to say that some attitudes and actions aren't inherently wrong. Some are. Bitterness, malice, dishonesty, and covetousness are wrong. So are stealing and slander. But sex isn't one of those things that are inherently wrong.

I've often wondered if Adam and Eve would have given much thought to the forbidden fruit if the Serpent hadn't spoken with Eve. One thing is for sure: he knew exactly what to say to make something off-limits look appealing.

Like an old friend, the Serpent asked Eve, "Did God really say, 'You must not eat from any tree in the garden'?" (Gen. 3:1).

Eve innocently told him that they could eat from any tree in the garden except one. She informed the Serpent that if they ate from that tree, they would die.

"You will not surely die. . . . Your eyes will be opened, and you will be like God," he assured her (Gen. 3:4–5).

Suddenly the fruit on that tree was the most desirable in the whole garden to Eve. The more she looked at it, the more appealing it became. Satan glamorized the forbidden fruit so it had a magnetic attraction.

Even though Eve had everything she needed, Satan deceived her into believing that she had needs God couldn't meet. He tricked her into thinking that if she would only eat the forbidden fruit, she would become like God.

Satan hasn't changed his line over the centuries. Today he tricks us into believing that sex with someone other than our wife will satisfy. It will give us what we really need.

While a one-night stand or an affair may bring great pleasure, that pleasure will be short-lived. Solomon said, "The lips of an adulteress drip honey, and her speech is smoother than oil; but in the end she is bitter as gall, sharp as a double-edged sword" (Prov. 5:3–4).

Solomon didn't deny the beauty of the other woman. Nor did he diminish the momentary pleasure she offers. Adam and Eve may have enjoyed the taste of the forbidden fruit. But that moment of pleasure was soon overcome by the consequences of their action.

Did the Devil Make You Do It?

We all know, at least on an intellectual level, that the pleasure of sin is momentary. But we're still vulnerable to the lie that tells us the forbidden fruit will deeply satisfy. We still want to taste its sweetness. And we'll struggle with the temptation to experience the other woman's beauty as long as we live.

The beauty of a man's wife has no bearing on the problem, either. I've known men who cheated on their wives even though they were married to professional models. Like Eve, we're always looking for something more, something that will give us more pleasure, more gratification. And like Eve, we're vulnerable to deception.

Why do forbidden things have such an appeal? In part because evil spiritual forces have the power to give them a glitter that attracts. Behind the scenes, there's something spiritual going on that we can't see. That's one reason the pull of lust is so strong.

Since Satan can glamorize sexual beauty that's off-limits, we might feel justified in blaming him for our struggle. Adam and Eve tried that approach when God confronted them with their sin. Adam blamed Eve, and Eve blamed the Serpent (Gen. 3:12–13). But God didn't buy it. He held the two responsible for their actions.

The Dragon Within

While Satan can tempt us, ultimately we make the choices. And when we choose to lust after forbidden beauty, our decision is driven by our own evil appetites.

On my eighth birthday my parents gave me a beautiful BB gun. Its cold steel barrel and carved wooden stock made it a thing of beauty. The gun and I formed a deadly partnership. Cans, bottles, road signs—nothing was safe from us.

Well, almost nothing. One afternoon I raised my gun and aimed at a bird perched in the willow tree in our backyard. Just as I was about to squeeze the trigger, my older sister, Patsy, ran into the yard waving her arms and yelling. As the bird fluttered away, she looked at me and smiled. She said nothing, but her smug face taunted, "Ha! Ha! Ha! Ha! Ha! I showed you who's in charge around here."

In that moment something inside took control. I lowered the barrel and aimed at my sister. A look of horror replaced her smug confidence, and she took off at a full run. I aimed at the part of her I considered most heavily padded and thought, "Sit on this!" as I pulled the trigger. The BB found its mark, and she grabbed her posterior and yelped. She darted into the house screaming, "I've been shot! I've been shot!" For a brief moment I wondered what had made me do something so cruel—then I realized how much I enjoyed it.

After my dad disciplined me, he confiscated my gun. But while he had the power to take away the tools I used for evil, he wasn't able to take away that dark side of my personality that enjoyed doing wrong.

All of us have areas in our lives in which we have at best mixed motives and at worst a strong downward pull. We know to do the right thing, yet we end up doing the wrong. The particulars of our inner battles may differ, but we all struggle with duplicity. We all enjoy doing what we shouldn't. We've all promised to reform, only to repeat the evil deed.[1]

I remember as a kid making up my mind to be good. But no matter how hard I tried, I still did things I shouldn't have done. As I matured, I learned how to cover my tracks. But even though others didn't know what was going on in my life, I knew. I knew there was a part of my personality that possessed an insatiable appetite for pleasure. And that dragon didn't care who it used or hurt.

The Dragon Awakens

Why do other women sometimes look better? Because of evil spiritual forces around us, and the dragonish, or sinful, appetites within us.

Of course, the dragon may hibernate. A man may pass through much of his life without a lust problem. Or the struggle may be so under control it's nothing to worry about. And then one day the man sees or experiences something that awakens the dragon from its slumber.

When that happens, we realize we're not the master in our own homes. We're the slaves. Our sinful nature has taken over. As the apostle Paul observed his own behavior, he concluded, "It is no longer I myself who do it, but it is sin living in me" (Rom. 7:17).

When Paul referred to himself as "I," he spoke of his core personality, that part of him that sought after God. He spoke of that place in his personality where God's Spirit lived.

Paul knew that his true self, the part of himself that was united with Christ, wasn't carrying out the wrong behavior. Instead it was his sinful propensity and its dragon-like appetites.

Don't misunderstand what Paul meant. He wasn't justifying his wrong actions. Nor was he shifting responsibility away from himself. Instead he was stating a fact. The true Paul, who so desired to do right, wasn't the one doing the evil. Instead it was the dragon who had gained dominion over him.

While I know Paul wasn't enslaved to sexual impurity, like everyone else he had the potential to be enslaved (Rom. 7:14–20). Even though he kept his sin under control, it continually tried to dominate him. He knew that the dragon within had the power to make him a prisoner. In fact, he said he knew what it was like to be its prisoner (Rom. 7:23).

About the Other Woman

You might think that knowing you shouldn't lust after other women will help you avoid the problem. It doesn't. In the garden, Eve knew what God wanted from her. But Satan actually used the commandment of God to tempt her. He asked her, "Did God really say . . . ?" (Gen. 3:1). That question was the starting place of her temptation.

Few things stir up our sinful appetites like the word "forbidden." For instance, what do you instinctively want to do when you're driving down an interstate and see a sign that says, "Speed Limit 55 mph"? Do you smile and say, "Oh, good"? I sure don't. No way! I want to disobey that law. I want to drive faster.

Nothing excites the dragon in your soul like a rule declaring something off-limits. That's why your dragon uses the laws of God to gain dominion over your life. That law will remind you that God said lust is wrong. You'll look at the commandment and know what you should do. You'll even tell yourself you're going to do the right thing. When you tell yourself that, the part of you that wants to do right enters into hand-to-hand combat with your sinful nature. And you don't have a chance.

That's what happened to David. He was a man who had it all. He had conquered his enemies and brought peace to Israel. David had a loving wife and close friends. He was not only a military genius but a poet. He penned many of the psalms as an expression of his love for God.

As a reward for his faith and faithfulness, God promised David a kingdom that would endure (2 Sam. 7:16). If anybody knew the right thing to do, it was David. Yet at a time when he should have been with his troops in the battlefield, David was at home. Instead of looking after his army, he was gazing at his neighbor and succumbing to temptation (2 Sam. 11:1–27).

Every time I read about David's fall, I wonder, "What was he doing on the roof of his palace, where he could see Bathsheba?" While I don't know for sure, I'd guess he was doing the same thing men today do when they channel surf while watching television in a hotel or when they thumb through an erotic magazine in a bookstore. He was checking out the other women—those he couldn't have.

Like other men, David wanted the woman God said was off-limits. Why? Because his sinful nature was aroused by the idea that he shouldn't or couldn't have her. And so is yours and mine. The dragon within us wants one thing: *total domi-*

nation of our lives (Rom. 7:23). And it will even use God's laws to enslave us.

That's Taboo

As I've addressed men's groups across the country and talked privately with other men, I've concluded that many Christian guys believe they're fighting a losing battle with lust. And it's a battle they don't feel free to talk about. Why? Because in Christian circles, sexual sins are serious—as they should be. But that legitimate seriousness can also create a fear of misunderstanding or rejection, and that fear often drives men to isolation. In every sense of the word, sexual sin is a taboo topic among Christian men.

That reality intensifies the problem of lust. Pornography, prostitution, and affairs all give the illusion of intimacy. The best way to combat that illusion is with real intimacy, or openness, with another person. Since most men haven't got that relational connection, the power of lust intensifies. Other women become irresistibly attractive because of the illusion of intimacy they provide.

The Bottom Line

"OK," you may be asking, "what's the bottom line here?" Let me review and then draw a conclusion.

We know that God created a mystery—men find a naked woman wonderfully beautiful. She looks real good to a man. But that mystery can quickly become dangerous, because men also find women other than their wife attractive. In fact, oftentimes it's the women we can't have who look the best. Why? Because

- evil spiritual forces glamorize them

- our sinful appetites are attracted to anything that's off-limits

- the law of God that commands us to flee immorality stirs up our lust

- the illusion of intimacy is often more compelling than reality

- we're isolated from other men and can't talk through our feelings

Hopefully, you now see why being a morally pure man is a serious challenge. This may have helped you realize why lust is such a big problem. The problem may even seem too big to overcome. But it's not. A number of years ago I heard a story that puts things in perspective.

The Incurable Itch

Once upon a time, a young man moved into a cave in the mountains to study with a wise man. The student wanted to learn everything there was to know. The wise man supplied him with stacks of books. But before he left the cave, the wise man sprinkled a powder on the man's hand that caused him to itch.

Every morning the wise man returned to the cave to monitor his student's progress. "Have you learned everything there is to know yet?" the wise man asked.

And every morning his student's answer was the same: "No, I haven't."

The wise man then sprinkled the itching powder on his student's hand and left.

This scenario was repeated for months. One day the wise man entered the cave, but before he could ask his question, the student reached out, grabbed the bag of powder, and tossed it into a fire.

"Congratulations," the wise man said, much to the student's surprise. "You have graduated. You know everything you need to know."

"How's that?" the student asked.

"You have learned that you don't have to wait until you've learned everything before you can do something positive," he replied. "And you have learned how to take control of your life and stop the itching."

It could be that your struggle with lust has created a relentless itch in your soul. You've scratched it, hoping it would get better. But it hasn't. Instead it demands more attention. You may have repeatedly promised yourself and God that you'd get your act together. But the itching persists, and you can't make it stop.

In a way, that's the aim of this book: to help you take control of your life and stop the itching. But the book's purpose goes beyond that. It seeks to help you become not just a man who can bridle his lust but a man who is morally pure, a man who lives his life in such a way that God looks at him and smiles. The chapters that follow will help you be that kind of man.

Thinking It Through

1. What role do evil spiritual forces have in a man's attraction to other women?

2. Why doesn't the presence of these demonic powers free us from responsibility for our actions?

3. Have there been times when you deceived yourself into believing you could enjoy sex outside of marriage and get away with it? What line of reasoning led to this distorted thinking?

4. What's the difference between appreciating a woman's beauty and lusting after her?

5. In what way do Christian churches and groups sometimes create an atmosphere that actually intensifies the
   problem of lust?

6. In what way does the other woman give the illusion of
   intimacy? How does that illusion differ from real intimacy? How can connecting with our wives and other men
   help us deal with this illusion?

7. Just as Satan glamorizes the beauty of a woman who is off
   limits, so God can enable a man to see his wife's beauty.
   Ask God to do that for you.

Chapter Three

I'm Caught and I Can't Get Loose

The day the story appeared in the *Oregonian*, Portland's major newspaper, I was having lunch with a friend. "What did you think of the fire at Adult Fantasy Video?" he asked.

Before I could answer, he said, "I feel sorry for the guy who died."

"Yeah, well, I feel sorry for his mother," I said. Reporters had interviewed her after the fire. She said she was sure he had only visited the video store a few times. He was a good son, a respected employee. "Imagine having that be the last memory of your son."

I have to tell you, I'm pretty shockproof. Few things surprise me anymore. But what my buddy told me next surprised me.

"It could have been me," he said.

"What do you mean?" I asked.

"I've been in that place. I've been in that room," he said. "Bill, you could have been reading about me in the paper today. You could be feeling sorry for my wife and kids."

"Are you ever going back?" I asked.

"I can't," he said. "It burned to the ground."

He's right, it did burn to the ground. But that's not the end of the story. The city slapped the owner's hand for a fire code violation, and his insurance company gave him a big enough settlement to rebuild the store. Now it's bigger and better than ever.

And what about my friend? I asked him a few weeks ago if he had visited the new store. He said he had. When I asked why, he said he didn't know why.

"Every time I leave that place, I feel like the scum of the earth," he said. "I swear I'll never go in there again. But later I just can't resist the urge. I'm caught and I can't get loose."

I wish I could say my buddy is unique. He's not. Some men can't resist the urge to watch adult shows on cable TV. Others can't say no to the pornography they find over the Internet. Others are pulled to the rush of an office affair or the thrill of a strip club.

It's easy to step into the trap of sexual lust. Getting out is another matter. The jaws of the trap are strong, its teeth sharp and long. In this chapter I want to examine the nature of sexual compulsions. I want to look at why they're so powerful. And I want us to understand the distorted thinking that drives them.

Turbocharged Lust

It would be nice if religious devotion freed us from the threat of sexual compulsions. It doesn't. Unfortunately, many churches actually create an environment in which sexual addictions thrive. Why? Because secrecy and risk increase the adrenaline rush associated with sexual sins. In a sense, they act like a turbocharger that infuses a man's lust with a powerful surge of energy.

The excitement of risk is present in a setting in which sexual sins are considered the worst of all vices. The greater the wrong, the greater the excitement associated with committing the wrong. Since sexual sins provide such excitement, they carry strong addictive power. And if a man commits a sexual sin, he'll probably keep it a secret. That makes the situation even worse. But most men would rather deal with the situation alone than run the risk of condemnation and rejection.

One authority in the field of addictive behavior told me he believed that fundamental Christians and religious leaders suffer from compulsive sexual behavior more than any other segment of society. Could he be right? Nobody knows for sure. But I do know that more Christians are hooked on sexual sins than most of us would imagine.

Over the past decade, I've conducted seminars in churches across the country. In an effort to take the spiritual pulse of these churches, I have frequently administered surveys. My aim wasn't to get an absolutely scientific read. I just wanted to get a feel for where the men were coming from. To my surprise, 55% of the men surveyed said they were struggling with a secret sexual addiction or had struggled with one in the recent past. The percentages were pretty much the same regardless of the setting or size of the church.

While most of these men were probably dealing with pornography and masturbation, others were dealing with more serious compulsions. Make no mistake about it, there are countless men attending church every week who live with the fear they'll be discovered. When the evening news shows pictures of men being arrested for picking up streetwalkers, they cringe in fear. Why? Because just the week before they had cruised the same neighborhood. Like my friend whose story I told at the beginning of this chapter, they know the news story could have been about them.

Risking It All

Sex is a favorite topic of afternoon talk shows. Montel Williams, Sally Jesse Raphael, and even Larry King regularly focus their shows on the escapades of somebody's sexual compulsions. The question they always ask is, "Why did you do it?"

As I write these words, I can't help but think of former presidential advisor Dick Morris. Just last week he made the rounds from one talk show to another, promoting his new book. As he gazed into the camera, Morris described his year-long affair with a Washington call girl. Without exception, every host asked the same question: "How could you have slept with a prostitute, when you knew it would cost you your marriage, your job, and your reputation?"

Morris, like most men when asked that question, didn't have a clear answer. "I don't know why I acted like a schoolkid," he said. "I had so much power, I thought the rules no longer applied to me."

Such answers skirt the issue. They don't get to the heart of the matter. While I don't know the specifics of each case, I do know one reason why men take such risks. They're hooked on adrenaline. In order to get an adrenaline rush, they have to increase the risk. When they were kids, just reading a *Playboy* magazine provided enough risk. After all, what would happen if their parents caught them? Now that they're adults, magazines don't provide nearly enough danger. They need to put all the chips on the table. They need to do something that will risk everything.

A He-Man with a She-Weakness

In many ways, the sordid stories we read about in our daily newspapers parallel the story of Samson. He was a great man. If he were alive today, his face would adorn the cover of *Sports Illustrated* as athlete of the year. Samson could do it all. He was faster than Michael Johnson, tougher than Mike Tyson. He was so strong, it's believed that the legend of Hercules was based on his exploits.

More important than his physical prowess was his spiritual strength. Samson was a man of God. He was "set apart to God from birth" (Judg. 13:5). As a symbol of his devotion to God, Samson never cut his hair. His long, flowing locks reminded people of his uncut commitment to God.

Samson was unique because God made him a conduit for his divine power. We are repeatedly told, "the Spirit of the LORD came upon him in power": before Samson slew a lion with his bare hands (Judg. 14:6); before he killed thirty Philistines single-handedly (Judg. 14:19); before he killed a thousand more Philistines with the jawbone of a donkey (Judg. 15:14).

Samson was respected as a godly man and a warrior. Yet although he was a he-man, Samson had a she-weakness. And that single flaw in his character proved to be his downfall. Samson was hooked on sexual experiences that were off-limits.

His first recorded words, spoken to his parents, revealed his problem: "I have seen a Philistine woman in Timnah; now get her for me as my wife" (Judg. 14:2).

How did his parents respond to that request? They pleaded with him to reconsider. They found it incredible that he couldn't find somebody God would approve of as a wife.

But Samson wanted the woman who was off-limits. His logic was simple: "She looks good to me" (Judg. 14:3 NASB).

Like anyone addicted to a sexual craving, Samson withdrew from his family and God. He chose the pleasures of the forbidden fruit rather than their company.

Tragically, Samson's marriage to the Philistine was cut short by her death.

Afterward he seemed to have bridled his sexual appetite for twenty years. But as he approached his fortieth birthday, his appetite broke free. Samson became sexually entangled with a Philistine woman, and it cost him his eyesight, his position, his reputation, and ultimately his life.

The Addictive Cycle

Samson was pulled into the addictive cycle. And I'm sure it contributed to his demise. If we could talk with Samson, I think he'd mention his midlife crisis. He had just turned forty and had done it all. He had crushed the Philistines and ruled Israel for twenty years. Sitting on top of the heap, Samson was bored. Having no goals, he was depressed.

The world's strongest man was vulnerable to something that would create a mood swing, something that would make him feel better fast. And nothing could change his mood like a beautiful woman—especially if that woman was off-limits.

There are four stages to the addictive cycle.

Preoccupation

In his boredom, Samson undoubtedly remembered his previous sexual adventure in Timnah. Soon he was preoccupied with thoughts of Philistine women. Just thinking about them created a mild rush of adrenaline. He enjoyed dreaming about an exciting night with such a woman.

Eventually he traveled to Gaza. He may have reasoned that he was "just looking." Soon he wandered into the red-light district. Afterward his fantasies became more vivid. Now he had the faces of the women he had seen. Now he could imagine the details of seducing them.

Preoccupation seems harmless enough. After all, nothing is actually done. While that's true, our thoughts are the seeds that germinate and grow into actions.

Ritualization

Rituals are activities we repeatedly do before acting out. When something excites us, we do it over and over again. We ritualize it.

For Samson, the rituals may have involved making return trips to Gaza or talking with prostitutes or dickering about their fees.

Like preoccupation, rituals seem harmless enough. They might involve channel surfing, browsing through a magazine rack at an airport, or reading ads for an escort service in the newspaper. The problem is, once we begin to ritualize, we will act out. It's certain.

I would imagine Samson struggled with his conscience. No wonder! He was Israel's spiritual leader. How did he justify his actions? He probably told himself Jewish women weren't exciting enough for a man like him. And besides, with a sex drive like his, how could one woman be expected to satisfy him?

Acting Out

Finally, during one of his trips, Samson stepped over the line. He slept with a Philistine prostitute (Judg. 16:1). While he was in her arms, Samson felt alive, more alive than he had felt in years. He felt young again. The pain of middle age was numbed. The old exhilaration was back. For years Samson had resisted the urge. Finally he gave into it. He unbridled his lust and let it run wild.

No matter how great the pleasure, the guilt quickly replaced it. The woman he felt he had to have he now wanted to run from. But no matter how far or fast he ran, Samson could not get away from the shame.

Shame

Soon guilt and shame washed away the pleasure. Samson had entered the woman's house boldly. He left under the cover of darkness, hoping nobody would see him (Judg. 16:3).

Repeating the Process

Samson probably vowed to stay away from Gaza. The men I talk with who have an affair or find self-pleasure in a hotel room while watching adult movies make similar vows. But when the pain of boredom or the pressure cooker of stress returns, so does their preoccupation with sex. That's certainly what happened to Samson. And having crossed over the line once, the second time was easier. Much easier. In fact, his sexual cravings were probably stronger than before. Again he went to Gaza and slept with a prostitute. And again he was overwhelmed with shame.

The story of Samson's sexual exploits illustrates the danger of repeating the four-stage addictive cycle. When the cycle is repeated,

- the addictive craving intensifies
- the craving for increased risk intensifies
- the desire to resist weakens

Like a deadly whirlpool that pulls its victims down, the addictive cycle can drag down the strongest man. Just ask Samson. It can overwhelm the most powerful. Just ask Dick Morris. In this chapter, I merely want to introduce you to the addictive cycle. In chapter 9, I'll help you devise a strategy to break free of its pull.

Addictive Thinking

While the addictive cycle explains what we do, it doesn't explain why we get hooked. Answering that question isn't easy, because different things cause men to become sexually compulsive. Yet there are at least four common threads of distorted thinking in each story of sexual addiction.

"I Can Regularly Experience the Exhilaration of Young Love"

After becoming a follower of Christ, I guarded myself from pornography. In fact, over a twenty-year period, I remember seeing only one pornographic image.

During the summer of 1988 I was staying in a motel in Phoenix, Arizona. It was hot outside and I was depressed. While channel surfing, I came across a partially nude female dancer. Like the night I gazed at my neighbor through her window, I was captivated. I wish I could say that was the last time I channel surfed during that trip. It wasn't.

When I returned to my home in Portland, Oregon, I discussed my experience with the guys in my group. By that time I was looking for something beyond the beauty of a woman's naked body to explain my feelings. As the men talked about similar experiences they'd had, I realized that the feelings we all described were like those of an infatuated teenager.

We laughed as we talked about our first love. I didn't have a problem remembering mine. There's something about a man's—or a woman's—first love that sets it apart. The first kiss. The first petting experience. Love awakens feelings and unleashes emotions that are new and powerful. It opens a whole new world to a man.

Of course, that first love seldom leads to an enduring relationship. Mine didn't. My girlfriend and I broke up, and a couple of years later I met Cindy. We fell in love, and once more I experienced the exhilaration of young love.

Over time that love grew. Cindy and I recently celebrated our twenty-fifth anniversary. We're fortunate, because we still love each other. Mature love is deeper and truer than young love. But it only occasionally possesses the feelings associated with infatuation and young love.

Many men believe that because they don't consistently experience the emotions associated with infatuation, they're no longer in love at all. They feel emotionally dead. A flirtatious coworker or a pornographic image on a computer monitor can stir up dormant feelings, feelings that were aroused when they were younger.

If a man is young and single, he may find himself pursuing the pleasure offered by pornography or strip clubs as vigorously as he would a woman.

The Law of Diminishing Returns

The first time a man becomes sexually active, he's participating in something that involves the law of diminishing returns. It takes more and more stimulation to get the same degree of pleasure. Initially a kiss excites. But soon it seems less exciting than what comes next—or what a man hopes will come next.

Once a man has seduced a woman, he has in a sense planted the flag. She is his—at least for the moment. The hunt, or pursuit, is over.

For many men, sex after marriage is boring. It's mundane. There's no challenge. There's no new terrain to explore. Even in the best of marriages, with the best possible sex, men still periodically struggle with such feelings. Deep down they long for the exhilaration of young love.

My experience in Phoenix infused me with an exhilaration that felt like young love. And like a kid in love, I wanted more. Of course, I faced a grave danger. In order to get the same rush, I would have to progress. The exhilaration of young love could be mine, but I'd have to view more explicit images. Eventually that would become boring, and I'd have to visit a video store or call an escort service or pick up someone in a bar.

Fortunately I cut the process off before it went any further. But not everyone makes that choice. Their hunt for the thrill of young love drives them to experience increasingly explicit and dangerous sexual experiences.

When women ask me, "Why is my husband so attracted to pornography?" I ask them, "Do you remember as a teenager when you first fell in love? Do you remember how good it felt to be with your boyfriend? Do you remember how you wanted to be with him all the time?"

Most women smile and say they do remember those feelings. "That's how your husband feels about pornography," I tell them. "It gives him the rush of young love."

"I'm a Bad, Unworthy Person"

This thought is at the core of all sexually compulsive behavior. It's hard to know whether it causes or results from an addiction. One thing is certain: after a man gives in to his sexual compulsions long enough, he begins to see himself as evil.

Men who step across the line of sexually inappropriate activity don't approve of their behavior. But once they see themselves as rotten at the core, acting out is easier. From their perspective, their evil behavior is consistent with their evil character.

These feelings of unworthiness are often cultivated in a man's family of origin. In the Old Testament, God repeatedly warned the Israelites that he would visit the sins of the fathers upon their children (Ex. 20:5; Num. 14:18). Nowhere is this more apparent than in the area of sexual compulsions.

Many men grew up in families that caused them to associate sex with shame. Men who struggle with visual sexual addictions often tell me they became hooked while reading pornographic magazines belonging to their father, grandfather, uncle, or other family member. Often their secret viewings were accompanied by masturbation, which was followed by feelings of shame. Not only does the attraction to pornography carry over into adult life, so does the shame.

Some men were sexually abused as children. These men usually have a deep sense of emotional dirtiness and shame that triggers a fear of abandonment. One reason they fear abandonment is often because parents who abused them threatened to leave if they told their secret. Researchers Eist and Mandel note that within families in which incest has occurred, "Tremendous parental threats of abandonment were a most frequent technique employed by the parent to control or immobilize their children."[1]

Boys who fear desertion feel unwanted. It's easy for them to think, "If I'm unwanted, I must be bad."

"No One Would Love Me If They Really Knew Me"

Because men feel safe with me, they frequently tell me things they're ashamed of. After listening to a painful confession, I'll frequently ask, "Have you told anyone else?"

All too often the response is simply, "No."

When I ask why, I'm told they don't have a friend, including their wife, who could handle it. In other words, they fear rejection. They can't imagine someone loving a person so defiled, so impure, so perverted.

Such feelings cause many men to conclude that

- real people can't be trusted

- real people won't meet their needs

- real people bring rejection and pain

In contrast to the suffering caused by real people is the pleasure provided by the object of their sexual compulsion. It never lets them down. It always gives a mood swing. It always brings pleasure. It always gives the illusion of intimacy.

"Sex Is My Most Important Need"

Men who grew up in abusive families sometimes turned to masturbation as a means of nurturing themselves. In a world of pain, they found something that made them feel better. Often the compulsive nature of their masturbation would reflect the emotional pain they were suffering. The greater the emotional pain, the stronger the drive to masturbate.

As boys, they equated sexual pleasure with love, care, and safety. As adults, whenever they experience pain they immediately turn to sexual pleasure as a means of coping and proving to themselves that they're OK.

For such men, nothing in life is more important than sex. They didn't bond with their parents when growing up, they bonded with sexual pleasure. Relational intimacy isn't as important to them as sexual pleasure. Indeed, nothing is as important as sex.

Getting Out of the Trap

Hopefully, as you've read this chapter you've gained a better understanding of compulsive sexual behavior and the distorted thinking behind it. But you may wonder exactly how big a problem you actually have. And you may want to know how you can find freedom.

In the next chapter you'll discover the scope of your problem. And you'll learn how you can pry open the teeth of the trap, pull out your soul, and take the first step toward freedom.

Thinking It Through

1. What are the four stages of the addictive cycle?

2. What are rituals? What are some of yours?

3. What are the three things that happen each time the addictive cycle is repeated?

4. How does sexual impurity involve the law of diminishing returns? Can you think of a time when you experienced this?

5. In what way does an off-limits sexual experience create the illusion of young love? What must a man do to keep that illusion alive?

6. Why would a man hooked on impure sex feel that others wouldn't love him if they really knew him?

Read Psalm 32 and reflect on how God deals with a man who confesses his sin (David had committed adultery and murder).

PART TWO

Admitting
the Struggle

Chapter Four

Raise the White Flag

If there's one lesson boys learn when growing up, it's the value of being tough, the value of winning.

Nowadays the heroes of the big screen portray the ideal man as rough and rugged. James Bond never gives up. Neither did the characters played by John Wayne. And Rocky always wins the big fight—or if he doesn't win, he at least "goes the distance." Those guys never gave up. And we don't want to give up either.

That resistance to raising the white flag serves men well during war or in a job situation that requires perseverance. It can help us hang in there when times are tough in a relationship. But when it comes to compulsive behavior, a refusal to give up only prolongs our agony. It leads to greater enslavement and harm.

Of course, most of us won't surrender until we know we're beaten or we know defeat is on the way. Maybe you're not convinced you even have a problem, or if you are, you're not sure how serious it is.

How to Know If You're Hooked

It's important to understand that sexual addictions don't happen overnight. They take time to develop. But when they're full-blown, a man won't be able to resist the repeated urge to enter into a love relationship with a sexual object or experience that gives him pleasure and the illusion of intimacy.

That last sentence defines an addict:

1. He's hooked and can't say no.

2. The object of his addiction gives him two things: pleasure and an illusion of intimacy.

Not everyone who struggles with sexual compulsions is an addict. Some men abuse their sexuality for a period of time and then grow out of it. Many men with a regrettable sexual experience in the past put it behind them and move on.

But not everyone is so fortunate. Some men block emotional pain with sexual pleasure. Over time they have to try increasingly risky forms of sexual behavior in order to deaden the pain. Eventually their world revolves around sex. Their obsession has taken over their life.

Patrick Carnes suggests a series of four questions aimed at helping us discover if we have a sexual addiction and if so, how far it's progressed.[1] While asking yourself these questions, it's crucial that you are brutally honest. The first step in dealing with a problem is admitting we have one.

Is Your Behavior a Secret?

Are you doing things you refuse to tell others about? Do you feel that if those closest to you knew what you were doing, they would reject you or strongly disapprove of your actions? Are you telling lies to cover your behavior? If so, you're isolating yourself from those you love and entering into a potentially addictive relationship with an object or event.

Is Your Behavior Abusive?

Does your sexual behavior create pain (emotional or physical) for you or others? Is it degrading or exploitative of others? Do you find yourself performing increasingly abusive acts? Do you derive pleasure from watching others being abused in some way?

Is Your Behavior Used to Deaden Painful Feelings?

Are your sexual actions an effort to change your mood rather than express affection? Do you masturbate or search for some other sexual outlet when you're depressed, bored, or angry? If your sexual behavior is used to erase pain, it's part of an addictive process.

Is Your Behavior Empty of Genuine Commitment and Caring?

Are you substituting the illusion of intimacy provided by an object or event for the genuine intimacy found in a healthy relationship?

If you answered yes to even one of the four questions, your sexual behavior is either compulsive or addictive.

Addictive Stages

While the four questions help determine if we have a problem, they don't tell us the extent of the problem. In order to determine that, we need to familiarize ourselves with the levels of addictions.[2]

Preaddiction

Preaddiction describes people who begin to find themselves sexually stimulated through impersonal objects, like pornography, or events, like strip clubs.

If you're at this level, your life is probably under control. You're holding down a job, and your relationship with your wife or girlfriend is intact. However, you realize that while your fascination with pornography, strip shows, or erotic talk lines isn't compulsive, it is dangerous. You may be troubled by the feeling that your slumbering lust could awaken and take over at any moment.

Level 1

At level 1 a man's lust has begun to exert its control. He's compulsively involved in such things as masturbation, pornography, homosexuality, or demeaning heterosexual relationships.

When a man reaches level 1, something significant has happened. While before he always struggled to keep his lust under control, now it's running wild. In his book *The Addictive Personality*, Craig Nakken notes that the single most important aspect of level 1 addictions is the emergence of the addictive personality.[3] A man's lust, like a great dragon, has awakened from its slumber and threatens to take over his life.

I experienced this the night I looked through my neighbor's window. It reminded me of the first time I got high on marijuana. I entered a new world and wanted to return to that world. There's something about that first high that people want to recreate. Similarly, a man who enters level 1 awakens his lust in a powerful way. And that initial experience is one he wants to recreate. When we enter level 1, the addictive part of our personality has been stirred. And make no mistake about it, the beast has an insatiable appetite that can slowly take over our life.

Level 2

When a man reaches level 2, he's taken a bigger and more dangerous step. Now his behavior involves victims and violations of the law. His activities include prostitution, exhibitionism, voyeurism, obscene phone calls, and touching a person intimately without consent. Most of the time he's considered more of a nuisance than a criminal, but unfortunately his behavior can inflict deep emotional pain on his victims.

Men who are exhibitionists or voyeurs will carry out their secret behavior for years. Living double lives, they're in constant fear of being caught.

All kinds of good people reach level 2. Hardly a week passes without a news story about a politician, teacher, professional athlete, or Hollywood star picking up a prostitute or making an unwanted sexual advance.

Level 3

By the time a man reaches level 3, his behavior involves serious crimes in which severe damage is done to the victim. Rape, incest, and child molestation occur at this level.

The Moment of Truth

By now you should know if you're hooked. You should also have a feel for how far your sexual compulsion has progressed. While most us would prefer avoiding the truth for as long as we can, eventually the moment of truth will arrive. Something will happen to force you to admit that your life is out of control.

- You'll accidentally leave a pornographic image on your computer monitor, and someone at work will report it to your boss.

- One of your kids will find your stash of X-rated videos.

- A policeman will arrive at your place of work because a neighbor has identified you as a Peeping Tom.

- Your wife will leave because you've had another affair.

- The school counselor will call because you've been reported to the child care agency for improperly touching a neighbor child.

For Samson, the moment of truth arrived near the end of his life. Blinded by lust, he slept in Delilah's lap while a Philistine barber cut his hair. A moment after the last strand fell, his enemies burst into his presence. Isolated from God, he was powerless to resist. Israel's champion became a bald-headed clown who entertained the Philistines.

Samson had fallen. He would never gaze at another Philistine woman. His enemies had made sure of that when they gouged out his eyes (Judg. 16:20–21).

Many people believe that Samson's story ends on a tragic note. I don't. Although he was blind and imprisoned, his hair began to grow, and so did his relationship with God. The Lord forgave Samson and used him one last time. The hero of Judah pulled down a Philistine temple, destroying himself and his enemies.

Samson learned firsthand what every man must know. God is the God of a second and third and fourth chance. He never gives up on us.

But to experience God's grace, we must first recognize our need. We must turn to him and others for help. That's not easy. Perhaps you now realize you have a problem but still believe you can handle it alone. As I mentioned at the beginning of this chapter, guys hate to admit defeat. We don't want to ask for help.

You Can't Overpower Your Lust

The apostle Paul understood our predicament. He told the Romans, "I have the desire to do what is good, but I cannot carry it out. For what I do is not the good I want to do; no, the evil I do not want to do—this I keep on doing" (Rom. 7:18–19).

I'm not suggesting that Paul struggled with compulsive sexual behavior, but he did struggle with sin—just like the rest of us. And like the rest of us, he would make up his mind not to commit a certain sin ever again. Did he succeed? No way! Now, if the apostle Paul couldn't overpower his sin, why should you and I think we can?

Even in a world free of erotic images, men don't control their lust. My oldest son called me last week from Pakistan. In that country men and women never hang out together. And women are covered with clothing from their head to their feet. Yet my son said he met a guy who offered to introduce him to some prostitutes.

If men in a country like that can't control their lust, how can we? From the moment we get up in the morning until we climb between the sheets at night, we're bombarded with erotic images and messages.

Suppose you made up your mind you were going to make it through one day without lusting after a woman. On your way to work your eyes are drawn to the bikini-clad model greeting you from a billboard. A few moments later as you stop at an intersection, you aren't able to keep from noticing the attractively dressed young woman crossing the street.

At work a friend brags about the gorgeous babe he bedded the night before. As you order lunch, the waitress with the short skirt winks at you and smiles. When you get back to the office, a coworker eagerly shows you his favorite erotic image on the Internet.

On your way home you stop at the grocery store and catch yourself gazing at the seminude models that adorn the magazines by the checkout counter.

When you finally get home, you plop down in an easy chair and flip on the TV. As you channel surf, you're exposed to more of the female anatomy than I found in the pages of *Playboy* when I was a kid.

With the high level of erotic stimulation you face on a daily basis, do you believe you can bridle your lust alone? I remember a friend once telling me (and he said this with a straight face), "I'll never have a problem with sexual lust."

I looked at him and said, "You're absolutely amazing. If that's true, you're stronger than Samson, godlier than David, and wiser than Solomon."

I'll never forget his response. He sat down and stared at me for a half minute without uttering a word. And then he said, "I never thought of it like that."

I'll guarantee you, if Samson, David, and Solomon were here, they'd all say, "You can't defeat your lust alone!"

You Can't Reform Your Lust

"OK," you may be thinking, "maybe I can't beat it. But I can make myself better. I can reform my lust."

I frequently talk with new Christians who think that becoming a follower of Christ means the lust problem is solved. It's as though they think Jesus waved some sort of magic wand over them and—presto!—their sinful nature was transformed. Their lust was gone.

When they discover that their problem with lust seems even worse than before, they decide they'll study the Bible and pray more. Much to their surprise, that doesn't seem to solve the problem, either.

Listen to Paul's words. In Romans 7:10–11 he said, "The very command that was supposed to guide me into life was cleverly used to trip me up, throwing me headlong."[4]

As we saw in chapter 2, our lustful appetites are so evil, they'll use God's good commands to tempt us. Like a rod stirring up dirt that has settled to the bottom of a jar of water, so God's law excites our lust. Forbidden things are more exciting. Women who are off-limits take on a greater appeal. God says don't and our lust says do. God says do and our lust says don't.

Trying to reform our lust is like trying to make a dog into a person. For thirteen years a buff-colored cocker spaniel named Pumpkin graced our family. Over those years I taught Pumpkin all kinds of tricks. She obeyed the common commands like sit, lie down, and roll over. I also trained her to jump through a hoop, close a door, sit on her hind legs, and fall over as though dead when I shot her with an imaginary gun.

Yet in spite of all my training, I couldn't keep Pumpkin from acting like a dog. She always did doggy things. She ate things people tried not to step in. She sniffed other dogs in places only dogs sniff. She went to the bathroom in public. No matter how well I trained Pumpkin, she was still a dog.

Similarly, your sinful propensity doesn't reform when you enter a church. It doesn't change when you come to faith in Christ. You can go to church, read your Bible, pray daily, and even lead a ministry without reforming your sinful nature. Paul said, "I know that nothing good lives in me, that is, in my sinful nature" (Rom. 7:18).

When we fall under the domination of our sinful nature, we're capable of doing anything evil, whether we're believers or not. When controlled by our lust, we can no more do good than a dog can talk.

Yet when dealing with their lust, men sometimes think they can reform it. They deny its evil power.

You may grow as a Christian. You may become more like Christ in your spiritual nature. But in the flesh, in your sinful nature, you're no better than the day you trusted Christ. And because your lust is driven by sin, you can't reform it.

You Can't Starve Your Lust

One of the problems I have with a lot of recovery programs is that their primary emphasis is on abstinence. They think the key to defeating an addiction is to stop the behavior. Now, please don't misunderstand me. We can't control any addiction unless we stop acting out. But if that's all we do, it won't work. We'll simply change addictions. For example, our lust will transfer from sex to alcohol. And if we stop drinking, it will move on to shopping or work or gambling.

It's impossible to starve our lust to death. Until the day we're with the Lord, we'll struggle with sin. A number of years ago I read a poem that describes the struggle and defeat we experience when we fight against our lust alone. While I don't know who wrote it, it's entitled "The Yipiyuk."

> In the swamplands long ago,
> Where the weeds and mudglumps grow,
> A Yipiyuk bit on my toe . . .
> Exactly why I do not know.
> I kicked and cried and hollered "Oh!"
> The Yipiyuk would not let go.
> I whispered to him soft and low.
> The Yipiyuk would not let go.
> Yes, that was sixteen years ago,
> And the Yipiyuk still won't let go.
> The snow may fall, the winds may blow.
> The Yipiyuk will not let go.
> I drag him 'round each place I go,
> And now my child at last you know
> exactly why I walk so slow.

Like the Yipiyuk, your sinful nature will resist letting go. For a while you may ignore it. Later you may insist it doesn't really have a hold on you. But if you hope to break its power, you must first realize it's there and admit you don't have the power to dislodge it.

Hopefully, you'll tire of fighting a losing battle. Paul did. In desperation he cried out, "Oh, what a terrible predicament I'm in! Who will free me from . . . this deadly lower nature?" (Rom. 7:24 LB).

If someone as spiritually together as Paul realized he was fighting a losing battle, isn't it time for you to do the same thing? I know giving up isn't easy. But it's a step you must take if you're going to find lasting freedom.

You may now begin to see your powerlessness to overcome your lust, and sense your need for God's help. In the next chapter we'll take the next step toward freedom.

Thinking It Through

1. What is an addict? What does the object of a man's addiction give him?

2. What four things indicate that a man is hooked? As you review these indicators, what do you learn about yourself?

3. What are the stages of an addiction? Where do you think you fit into these stages? Why?

4. Why can't you overpower or reform your lust?

5. What is the advantage of realizing you can't beat your lust, no matter how hard you try? Have you reached that point? If not, why not? If you have, why?

Chapter Five

Drag It into the Light

We've all been embarrassed.

One of my more embarrassing moments occurred while I was addressing a large group of high school students in Northern California. As I spoke, the group would laugh at inappropriate times. Because I use a lot of humor when I speak, I initially figured that their laughter was the residue of a story I had told. But when the inappropriate laughter continued, I figured my fly must be open. I tried to nonchalantly do a zipper check. That didn't work, so I just held my Bible in front of the barn door and figured it would keep them from looking in.

When I finished speaking, I was surprised to discover that my pants were zipped. Several students gathered around me and began asking questions. Before I answered them, I had one of my own. "Why were you all laughing throughout my talk?"

"Oh," one of the girls said with a giggle, "because of your Texas accent."

Toxic Shame

We've all seen people do things that embarrassed them—they've stumbled or spilled food all over themselves or forgotten someone's name. The shame associated with such embarrassment is healthy. It reminds us we're human and keeps us from taking ourselves too seriously. But there's another kind of shame that's toxic. It's like radioactive waste that destroys its container.

This kind of shame has to do with who we are as men. It's based on the belief that we've failed God and ourselves. This shame is different from guilt. Guilt addresses behavior. It has to do with what we've done. Guilt is a painful feeling about our actions. Shame is a painful feeling about who we are as a person. It exists when *we're* wrong. Shame involves our being, our core identity. A shame-driven man holds himself in contempt. He believes he can't be trusted. He not only guards against exposing himself to others but resists exposing himself to himself. He's afraid to look at himself too closely, for fear of what he'll see.[1] Shame-driven men are alienated from God, themselves, and others.

Because shame creates alienation and pain, many shame-driven men quickly latch onto a sexual object or experience that replaces their pain with pleasure and provides an illusion of intimacy. The problem is, every sneak peek at a "men's" magazine, every visit to the adult video store, every one-night stand, and every affair merely creates a greater sense of unworthiness. This increased shame and pain intensifies the need to feed the addictive appetites in order to deaden the pain and replace the feelings of aloneness with false intimacy.

In my early twenties I used to smoke marijuana and chase girls to deaden the pain of my shame-based loneliness and hurt. The problem is, the more I acted out with drugs and sex, the more ashamed I felt. I had to have more dope and more sex to feel OK about myself.

When I became a devoted follower of Christ, my lifestyle changed. But my feelings of shame didn't just go away. I remember not wanting to have kids for years after I got married, because I feared they'd grow up and be like me. I was a flawed person, and even though I wasn't acting out, I believed my lust would eventually gain the upper hand again.

Facing Our Shame

Nobody likes to deal with their shame. Approaching it is like climbing into a cave with a sleeping bear. The best we can hope for is a bad scare. But if we actually grab hold of the bear, things could be much worse. The bear might rip us to shreds. Most men feel ill-equipped to take on such a beast. So they avoid the cave and the bear. Ultimately, it's fear that keeps us from facing the truth about ourselves.

That's what happened to Adam and Eve. Before the Fall they were "both naked, and they felt no shame" (Gen. 2:25). What a statement! They had nothing to hide from each other. Adam and Eve experienced untainted intimacy with God and each other.

And then sin entered the picture. Their wrongdoing caused them not only to suffer guilt but to become spiritually scarred. Their inner person was stained. At their core they were now sinful.

How did they respond? First they experienced fear—fear that God would see their sin, fear that they would be rejected. Next they hid from each other and from God. Finally, when confronted with their sin, they evaded responsibility by blaming someone else. Adam blamed Eve and Eve blamed the Serpent.

Like Adam and Eve, we all frantically try to cover up our shame. We try to find someone or something else to blame for who we are and what we've done. As long as we succeed in hiding our shame, we remain its slave.

Fortunately, God refused to allow Adam and Eve to stay in hiding. He chased them down and dragged their guilt and shame into the light. He exposed what they had been trying so hard to hide. Then, and only then, did they find intimacy with him and with each other.

The Battle behind Our Shame

Of course, we know something Adam and Eve didn't know. We know they were the key players in a struggle between good and evil, a battle between God and Satan. The only question that mattered was who would win domination over their souls.

Satan uses the fear of rejection and abandonment to keep us from dragging our sin into the light. He shackles us with shame so we feel too unworthy and unlovable to let others see what we're really like. The sin and shame, or our attempt to hide our guilt, then takes precedence over our love relationships with God and other people.

It's bad enough that we feel shame over what we've done, but matters are far worse than we think. Why? Because our obsession with immorality is a form of idolatry. When I address men's groups, I try to help them see this awful truth. We tend to think of an idol as some sort of golden image in the shape of a man, woman, or animal. But an idol is anything we trust besides God to meet our deepest needs. Paul said that behind every idol is a demon (1 Cor. 10:18–20). Ultimately, when we give ourselves to an object of sexual lust, we're embracing the demon behind the object.

Grabbing the Grace of God

When we refuse to drag our shame into the light, we suffer a greater tragedy. Jonah said, "Those who cling to worthless idols forfeit the grace that could be theirs" (Jonah 2:8).

I don't know about you, but I don't want to miss out on the grace of God. I don't want to be like the kid who slipped his hand into an expensive vase. When he couldn't get it out, he ran screaming to his mother. She tried everything, from liquid soap to a firm tug, to free his hand. Nothing worked. When the boy's dad finally got home, he gently cracked the priceless heirloom with a hammer. As the shattered vase fell away, the boy stood with a clutched fist.

Shocked, his mother asked, "Why didn't you open your hand so we could get it out of the vase?"

The child uncurled his fingers and revealed a silver coin. He stared at it, and with tears streaming down his cheeks, he said, "I was afraid I'd drop my quarter."

Like that boy, we sacrifice the vase of God's grace when we hold on to an object of our lust.

You don't have to forfeit God's grace. You can let go of the idol you're holding on to. How? By dragging your shame into the light.

Stop Playing Dodgeball

Dragging our shame into the light means we need to stop avoiding the truth about ourselves. As a kid, I used to enjoy playing dodgeball. I was quick and could evade almost any ball. If I couldn't avoid it, I'd catch the ball and throw it at an opponent, and he'd be out.

I think most men have mastered the game of spiritual dodgeball. We've become expert at evading responsibility and throwing it at someone or something else. By dodging responsibility, we hope to avoid the suffering that occurs when we see and embrace our sinfulness.

In his book *People of the Lie,* M. Scott Peck describes people who are dedicated to maintaining an appearance of moral purity. They're aware of their own evil but are frantically trying to avoid that awareness. He defines an evil person as someone who is "continually engaged in sweeping the evidence of their evil under the rug of their own consciousness."[2]

Tragically, since evil people want to dodge, or disguise, their evil, they're often found involved in churches.[3] Why? Because by cloaking themselves with the robe of religious activity, they can conceal from themselves and others the true nature of their soul.

I mentioned earlier the shock I experienced when I discovered that two of the key leaders in my church had been watching their neighbor through a window. They had successfully led small groups and served on the board of the church without anybody guessing what they were doing. Some men carry out a double life for decades.

Facing Our Dirty Secrets

Of course, as sinners, we're all contaminated with evil. We're all capable of doing just about anything. The question is, what will we do about it? Will we keep dodging the truth, or will we stand still and embrace it? If we embrace it, we'll have to face those nasty secrets about our family and ourselves.

- Secrets about physical and sexual abuse

- Secrets about alcoholism and brutal family fights

- Secrets about other addictions and the grave consequences that flow from them

- Secrets about imperfections you never talk about

- Secrets about your own sexual behavior

These secrets are the source of your shame. They are the reason you don't believe anybody would love you if they really knew you. They are the reason you keep others, even those closest to you, at an arm's distance.

Assuming Responsibility

It's important to realize that those secrets aren't excuses. They don't justify our behavior. They're simply the painful truth about our past and present. They are part of the reason we're filled with shame. Not only must we face those secrets, we must identify how and when we've blamed others for our predicament.

We all need to realize that

- our parents aren't to blame for our situation

- our wives aren't to blame for our destructive sexual behavior

- the pornographers, prostitutes, and dancers aren't to blame for our lust

We are. And that is the simple but painful truth.

Three Lists

Take some time right now, or whenever you can find a quiet, private place, and write out three lists. First, identify every shameful secret you can think of. Second, write out every excuse, justification, and rationalization you've made for your behavior. Third, identify those people you've blamed for your current situation.

Making these lists is crucial. It enables you to identify those memories that you've hidden, memories that feed your shame. It enables you to stop blaming your circumstances and other people for your problems. Once you've made the lists, you're ready for the next step.

Tell God What You've Done

So far you've seen your stuff. Now it's time to show it to someone else. I always encourage men to begin by bringing it to God. He's already aware of what you've done. He's acquainted with your shame.

Nobody illustrates better what you need to do than the Prodigal Son (Luke 15:11–32). If anybody had reason to fear rejection and abandonment, it was him. Itching to indulge his lustful appetites, he demanded his share of his father's inheritance. By doing that, the prodigal was telling his father he wished he were dead. He made it clear he valued his father's money more than his father.

With his pockets filled with cash, he took off and never looked back. Why should he? In the "distant country" he had lots of friends, beautiful women, and plenty of wine. His every fantasy became a reality.

And then he ran out of money. Without money to entertain his friends, they deserted him. Eventually he ended up feeding pigs. He became so miserable that he longed to eat pig food.

The prodigal bottomed out. And it was there he came to his senses. Filled with shame, he decided to return home. As he made the journey, he rehearsed his lines. He reviewed every sin he had committed against his father.

He was at the same place you may be. And like you, he wasn't sure how his father would respond. What he discovered about his father is what you'll learn about God.

Your Heavenly Father Loves You

The ancient religious Jews believed God hated sinners. That's why they felt disdain for Jesus. He hung out with prostitutes, dishonest businessmen, and crooked politicians. Jesus loved sinners. And so does his Father.

No matter what filthy pigpen you've climbed into, you're never so dirty that God doesn't love you. Right now he's waiting for you to come to him. The prodigal's father ran down the road to greet him. He embraced his wayward son and kissed him.

Of course, the purpose of the story was to illustrate how God feels about people like you and me, people who have turned their backs on him and done stupid and sinful things, things they're ashamed of, things they want to hide from.

Your Heavenly Father Accepts You

It's impressive to me that the father embraced his son and kissed him. But he did more than that. He restored the prodigal to a position of honor and influence.

One thing men fear, in addition to rejection and abandonment, is uselessness. We fear we've done something that will relegate our lives to the wastebasket. We wonder how God could possibly use someone who has done what we've done.

Last night I was reading the story of Peter's denial of Jesus. The Lord predicted that three times Peter would deny knowing him. And then Jesus said, "I have prayed for you, Simon, that your faith may not fail. And *when you have turned back, strengthen your brothers*" (Luke 22:32). What a statement! Jesus knew what Peter would do, and yet he spoke of Peter's future usefulness.

The prodigal's father gave his son a robe, a ring, and sandals, because he accepted him completely—no holding back. He would have the honor of a son and do the work of a son.

The same is true of you. In spite of what you've done, God accepts you. Your heavenly Father has work for you to do.

Your Heavenly Father Celebrates His Relationship with You

What a party! The father prepared a banquet, brought in a band, and invited everyone he knew. Why? Because he was overjoyed that his son was back home.

I love this story. But I wonder what would have happened if the boy had never returned home because he believed his father would reject him. How tragic that would have been. And how tragic it would be for you to make that same mistake.

The moment you bring your lists to God, he will initiate a celebration in heaven like you've never seen. Nothing gives him more pleasure than his relationship with you. And nothing will give him greater joy than for you to drag your shame into the light of his presence so he can forgive you, cleanse you, and prepare you for future use.

Accept Yourself As God Does

Of course, the healing of our shame doesn't occur instantaneously. You'll still struggle with the fear of rejection and abandonment. Since you may relapse, thoughts of self-condemnation can overwhelm you. You may say to yourself, "It's no use. I'm too far gone to deal with this" or "There you go again! You've confessed your sin and shame to God and done the same thing all over again. You're no good!"

It's crucial for you to recognize that those thoughts are coming from your sinful nature and Satan. It's an attempt to feed your shame so you'll pull away from God and other people. Remember, one of Satan's primary roles is to accuse God's people so they'll be overwhelmed by guilt and shame (Rev. 12:10).

The way to counteract such lies is with the truth. Doing so involves a choice. You must choose to tell yourself, "God unconditionally loves me, and I receive his love and love myself." Whenever you're alone, say this out loud. Say it often! For years you've probably been telling yourself that you're a terrible person. It will take time to change the way you view yourself.

There's nothing you can do to make yourself more lovable to God. He wouldn't love you more if you were perfect. And he doesn't love you less because you're imperfect. You're loved just as you are. If you refuse to believe you're loved, you're calling God a liar. You're implying that you can determine your value better than God can. Are you ready to say that? I hope not. It's not just unwise, it's destructive.

Saying, "God loves me and I accept his love" counteracts the voice of shame. Each time you repeat that, you're tapping into the love of God. And his love has the power to transform you.

But you must choose to accept his love and allow him to transform your self-image. You can choose to flood your mind with shameful thoughts that cloud your identity. Or you can say, "God loves me and I am his child." As you acknowledge God's love, you'll begin to see yourself as he does.

Putting Your House in Order

The process of personal change occurs over the course of our lifetime. Now that you've dragged your shameful secrets into the light, the next step involves dealing with the destructive system around you that fosters your sexually compulsive behavior. Part of that system has to do with your family of origin (the family you grew up with) and the destructive roles you learned there. In the next chapter you'll identify those roles and discover how to break free from them.

Thinking It Through

1. How is a sexual obsession a form of idolatry?

2. What are the dirty secrets in your life you want to keep hidden? Have you ever told anyone about them? How do you think they would respond if you told them? Have you ever brought them to God? How would he respond if you did?

3. Write out the three lists described in this chapter. Once you've done that, tell God what you've done.

4. How does it affect you to know that your heavenly Father loves you, accepts you, and celebrates his relationship with you?

Chapter Six

Your Family of Origin

As the class clown, I had a bad habit of saying the wrong thing at the wrong time. My inappropriate sense of humor plagued me through high school, college, and into graduate school.

Of course, we all like to make others laugh. At times we all want to clown around. My problem was, I allowed my role as the class clown to define me. It had become a cocoon that protected me. I could win friends by being funny. And I could keep people away with the same technique. Of course, there was a price. Teachers tended to frown at my antics. And some people I wanted to impress viewed me as immature—out of control.

Most of us learned specific roles while we were young, roles that were produced in part by the dysfunctional families in which we grew up. (By "dysfunctional" I mean families that didn't function in the way God intended.)

What I'm talking about is a codependent role we assume while growing up. There was a time when the word "codependent" confused me. I thought a codependent was always the husband or wife of an alcoholic, someone who in some mysterious way was also dependent on alcohol.

Actually, that definition is partially right. When psychologists and sociologists first started examining the families of alcoholics, they discovered that every drunk had someone who helped them stay that way, a person who would call their boss and tell them they couldn't come to work because they were sick (of course, they were really hungover), or would bail them out of jail when they were arrested for driving under the influence of alcohol.

Instead of letting an alcoholic bottom out, codependents come to the rescue. In doing so, they became so obsessed with the alcoholic's behavior, they neglect what is going on in their own life.

For a long time a codependent was seen as the spouse of an addict. And then researchers learned something significant. They discovered that *every* member of a family is affected by an addict's behavior. Every adult and child assumes a role aimed at controlling the addict and bringing balance to the family.

A Family Album

How do we become codependent? As children, we learn unwritten rules for relating to other people. Children raised in dysfunctional families learn to react to the primary stressor in the family. This could be a parent who has an alcohol or work addiction, inflicts physical or verbal abuse, tries to control everyone's feelings, enforces religious rigidity, or commits sexual abuse.[1]

Before the addiction the family is in balance. When a shift in the balance occurs, each member finds the imbalance intolerable. They individually adapt to the stress that caused the shift, in an attempt to control it and restore balance. As long as the stress exists, family members live in a constant state of readiness to cope with it. Over time each one assumes a codependent role in the family.

For instance, in a stress-filled family, one child may assume the role of the *family hero*. This child is out to save the family name. Family heroes are usually driven to excel in everything they do. As adults, they often become workaholics in "helping fields" such as medicine, social work, or church work.

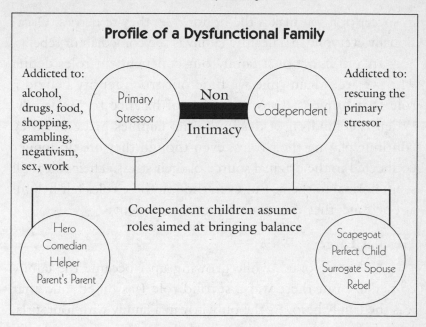

Profile of a Dysfunctional Family

Addicted to: alcohol, drugs, food, shopping, gambling, negativism, sex, work

Primary Stressor

Non Intimacy

Codependent

Addicted to: rescuing the primary stressor

Hero
Comedian
Helper
Parent's Parent

Codependent children assume roles aimed at bringing balance

Scapegoat
Perfect Child
Surrogate Spouse
Rebel

Another child will take on the role of the *comedian* to provide comic relief for the family. Comedians divert attention from the real issues by clowning around and attracting attention to themselves.

One child may become the family *scapegoat*. Scapegoats detract attention from the problem with inappropriate and sometimes antisocial behavior. Scapegoats need attention and get it with their behavior.

The *perfect child* in the family is the forgotten child, the one nobody has to worry about. Perfect children express no needs and are rewarded for it.

Other roles children may assume in dysfunctional families include the *helper,* the *surrogate spouse,* and the *parent's parent.*

In a healthy family everyone plays different roles at different times. When the dad makes a big sale and treats the family to dinner, he's the hero. When a daughter scores a winning goal in soccer or a son makes the honor role, they're heroes. Occasionally everyone in a healthy family is the comedian or rebel.

In a dysfunctional family our codependent roles define who we are. Meanwhile we hide our true identity behind a role that brings a distorted sense of balance to the family. When the children of dysfunctional families grow up, they continue playing their roles, even though they are no longer connected to the original source of their stress. Their roles still seem normal to them. But even though these roles felt helpful at one time, they eventually become destructive.[2]

Hero at Large

As I mentioned, while growing up I became the family comedian. But there was a second role I assumed, and that was the family hero. As the only boy in a family with four girls, I was expected to excel at everything I tried—especially sports. Since that was the case, I had to be tough and competitive. For that to happen, I had to let go of my feelings of compassion, fear, and vulnerability. Obviously, I wasn't aware that I had assumed a codependent role. I certainly didn't think I had a problem. On the contrary, I viewed myself as a highly competitive and competent person.

I could tell numerous stories about people I've tried to rescue. Don't misunderstand me—I'm not talking about offering guidance to people in need or assisting people who ask for help. I'm talking about being driven to rescue people I thought had great potential. I'm talking about assuming responsibility for the success of people I didn't think could make it without me, people like Kent.

One afternoon Kent, who looked like the cowboy in the Marlboro ads, dropped by my office. "I'm building a first-class athletic club in Houston," he drawled. "It's going to be the nicest club in town."

"How long have you lived in Houston?" I asked.

"I moved here several months ago from Arkansas. I had several clubs there. Before that I owned clubs in Louisiana and Georgia."

"How did you get into the athletic club business?"

Kent sat up in his chair. He flashed a broad smile. "I used to be a professional boxer. I got into the business while training as a fighter. Later I wanted to get into movies, but it didn't work out. I got strung out on alcohol and drugs. A few years ago I came to the Lord. He's really made a difference."

The more Kent talked, the more I liked him. Kent was dynamic and influential. I saw tremendous potential in him.

For almost a year I tried to get together with Kent every week. He said he wanted my help, so I gave it to him. He wasn't very reliable about keeping appointments, but I continued to meet with him. Even though he indicated no willingness to change, I didn't give up on him. I imagined what he would be when he got his act together. I intended to be the person to help him find out what he could become.

One morning Kent failed to show up for a breakfast appointment. It wasn't the first time. But on this occasion he sent his business partner. That was the day I learned why Kent had shattered two marriages, run through several successful businesses, and occasionally stood me up.

Kent was strung out on coke. He had been for years.

Amazingly, he had surrounded himself with people who covered for him, put up with his lack of consideration, kept him from being responsible for himself, and added dignity to his lifestyle.

As I left that breakfast appointment, I felt used. I was angry at Kent. He obviously didn't appreciate the sacrifices I had made for him, nor had he taken my advice.

How did I respond? I withdrew. I persecuted him by cutting him off emotionally. Kent retaliated by accusing me of not being there when he needed me. Suddenly I had become the victim.

Who's the Victim, Anyway?

I've told that story because it illustrates how my childhood role as the family hero carried over into my adult life. I wanted to help Kent more than he wanted to be helped. The story also shows how a codependent can become over time both the persecutor and the victim.

Stephen B. Karpman compares the roles a codependent plays to the three points of a triangle. First, we rescue people. Second, we get mad and persecute them when they don't respond the way we want them to. Finally, we feel used and end up being punished by the person we tried to rescue. We become the victim.[3] I acted out all three roles with Kent and with others.

Until I began to understand codependency, I never knew why I was attracted to troubled people with great potential. I didn't understand why I continued trying to rescue them after they dumped on me. Too often my motive wasn't to honor God. The payoff for me was the emotional pleasure I derived from rescuing someone. I liked the thought of being someone's hero. It made me feel good, just like when I was a kid and could be a hero to my family.

Codependency in the Church

I'm convinced the church nurtures codependent relationships. At times we even inadvertently train people to be codependents. We teach, as we should, that self-sacrifice is the highest form of love. The problem is, people learn how to *act* lovingly and sacrificially without *being* loving. Codependents are really helping themselves. They enjoy the feeling of power they have during the rescue. They feel righteous and good about helping others. Unfortunately, such rescuing is a subtle form of self-glorification.

And what happens when the persons being rescued don't respond as expected? Codependents become angry. They feel they've been taken advantage of. They persecute, and then they become the victims.

It's easy to forget that rescuing people is God's job. We're simply to share his love. We're here to help people who are willing to be responsible for themselves.

My attempts at rescuing people who weren't ready to be rescued never helped anybody. On the contrary, they actually slowed their growth by protecting them from the consequences of their actions. Most people refuse to change until they experience the painful repercussions of their bad choices. God never relieves people of their responsibility for their actions, and neither should we.

Destructive Actions

Behavior that helped us survive as children doesn't go away easily. Even though the original cause of our behavior is gone, we tend to continue acting in the same way. After all, it seemed to work in the past. But it doesn't work in the present. In fact, when we're acting in a codependent role, our behavior is often harmful. Consider the following behaviors and how destructive they can be.

Reacting

When we react, we are immediately and thoughtlessly pulling in the opposite direction to another person. We feel things are out of balance, and we react to get them in balance.

When King Saul discovered his son Jonathan has disobeyed a command not to eat honey, he reacted. Instead of

acting with a well-thought-out response, the king pronounced
a death sentence on Jonathan. While the rest of the troops
changed Saul's mind, the eratic king consistently reacted without thinking (1 Sam. 14:24–45).

Adults who grew up in a family that went from one crisis
to another learn to react. Sometimes we react because we're
embarrassed by the behavior of another person. If either of
your parents was an alcoholic, you know the embarrassment
you felt when a friend saw your parent drunk. When something like that happens, we want to fix the damage the other
person's behavior caused. We want to shield them and ourselves from what happened.

Controlling

Codependents try to control others. Several years ago I
counseled a couple, Jay and Kip. Jay had an addiction to both
alcohol and sex. Every couple of weeks he would drink too
much, visit nude bars, or watch pornographic movies. Kip did
all kinds of things to try to control his addictions. She super-
vised him, went out in the evenings and searched for him,
called all over town, forced him to go to a counselor, searched
his clothes for clues, and yelled at him.

Kip did all of this in the name of love. She said she was
only trying to help. On the outside she appeared sweet and
caring. She said she just wanted her husband to obey God.

On the inside Kip was desperately trying to force her husband to bow to her will. She felt it was her job, not God's, to fix
him. She refused to let go of the reins and allow the man's life
to follow its natural course. She refused to move aside and allow
God to make him so miserable he would want to change.

Did Kip's controlling behavior do any good? Of course
not! It never does. Instead of controlling her husband, she was
actually placing herself under his control.

After some extensive reading and painful counseling, Kip released her husband to God. Slowly he began to change.

Even if he had never changed, Kip needed to let go. Otherwise her husband would have continued to resist her control. He would have repeatedly punished her for making him do things he didn't want to do.

Rescuing

What prompts us to keep trying to rescue people who in turn make us their victims? As with other addictions, a poor sense of identity drives much of our behavior. Often children who grow up in dysfunctional families fear abandonment. They don't receive the affirmation and nurturing needed to make them feel safe and secure. Consequently, they believe something is wrong with them.

In order to feel worthwhile, they'll do anything. Early on they learn that taking care of others in the family makes them indispensable. Therefore they'll be a clown, a hero, a perfect child, or a rebel. Their role makes them valuable. Codependency drives us to find our identity in other people instead of in God.

Negative Emotions

The next time you find yourself trying to rescue someone by playing your codependent role, watch for a shift in your mood. If you feel used because the person you're trying to help doesn't respond the way you want or fails to express appreciation, your motives for helping them may have been self-serving. You were likely trying to rescue them so you would feel better about yourself rather than because you genuinely care for them.

The following emotions may alert you that you're functioning in your codependent role.

Disappointment

Perhaps the greatest emotional pain a codependent experiences is the pain of disappointment. The life you hoped for and worked for never materialized. The person you slaved for turned against you.

I understand such disappointment. Years ago a young man, Sean, joined the staff at the church of which I was the senior pastor. Seldom have I clicked so quickly with another person. He was the brother I never had. The two of us dreamed about a lifetime of ministry together. In a short time he built a thriving youth ministry in our church.

As our friendship grew, Sean became more abrasive with me. I told myself he was immature and just needed more time. After all, nobody's perfect. I wasn't worried because, as a hero, I knew I could help him.

Occasionally friends pointed out to me that Sean's problems were more severe than I thought. People who had known him in his previous ministry warned me about him. When I talked with him about what I had heard, he said these people were lying.

It was easy for me to trust Sean. I had learned as a child to see the best in people, especially people with serious problems.

Late one night I received a phone call from another pastor, informing me that Sean was sexually involved with a single girl. Heartbroken, I confronted my friend. Rather than accepting my help, he turned against me. The rescuer became the victim again.

Others have seen their dreams of a loving marriage shattered by an alcoholic spouse who refused all help. Parents have suffered the disappointment of a child hooked on drugs who rejects them and everything they have to give.

Certainly, we should grieve our losses. It would be unloving and inhuman not to suffer pain after such disappointments. But a codependent has a way of searching out relationships that will end in disappointment.

Guilt

One reason we persist in our efforts to help other people is because we feel responsible for their failures. Since we're trying to rescue them, we blame ourselves when they don't get better. We feel guilty.

Obviously, there are times when we should feel guilty. If we've done something wrong, our conscience should tell us. When it does, we need to confess our sin to God and accept his forgiveness (1 John 1:9).

On other occasions we experience false guilt—that is, we feel we've done something wrong when we haven't. Inappropriate guilt occurs when something happens that's beyond your control.

When a child tries to save a parent's marriage and it ends in divorce, the child may feel responsible. He isn't. When Sean sinned, I felt responsible.

Unresolved guilt can result in self-hatred and shame. Such thoughts and emotions can drive us to try harder to help someone who doesn't want to be rescued.

Anger

When disappointment and guilt aren't properly dealt with, they can lead to anger. I'm not talking about justifiable anger. When we see an injustice, we should feel anger. It may prompt us to do something to right a wrong.

The kind of anger codependents often experience results from years of disappointment and guilt. It's an unhealthy anger that occurs because an expectation hasn't been met. Codependents feel they've lost something of value.

When this kind of anger is suppressed, it causes ongoing feelings of rage. Periodically this anger will explode. I've witnessed violent and frightening outbursts of anger when an addict refuses to bow to the demands of a codependent.

Some codependents are too controlled to have a violent outburst. Instead their anger seeps out like acid. They use sarcasm to bite away at the person who has resisted their rescuing attempts.

Codependency and Sexual Compulsions

It may be that this chapter has helped you see how growing up in a dysfunctional family has caused you to adopt a codependent role or roles aimed at helping others, at bringing balance to a situation. But you may be having a hard time linking your codependency to your sexual compulsions. I've identified two ways they are tied together.

First, unresolved disappointment, guilt, and anger can lead to self-hatred and shame. As we saw in the last chapter, shame often compels us to seek relief in harmful ways. And once we start seeking, there are plenty of sexual experiences available that can give us a quick mood swing.

Second, your codependent roles hide the real you. As a hero, I felt I always had to win. I always had to rescue family members, church members, and friends. As a hero, I learned to conceal my feelings of disappointment, rejection, failure, and abandonment. I appeared confident and tough, even in the face of pain and disappointment.

As a comedian or clown, I always tried to be funny. I learned how to turn the most painful situation into a joke. As an adult, my sense of humor serves me well. But it can easily become a shield that keeps friends from getting close enough to see my pain and help me deal with it.

As we'll see in chapter 11, a key to lasting purity is the development of intimate, open, authentic friendships. As long as we're relating to people as an actor playing a role, they'll never see the real us. And they'll never be able to help us cope with our pain in healthy ways.

Finding a Way Out

Working through codependent behavior requires both understanding and effort. Spend time thinking about the role you had in your family while growing up. Look at your present relationships and see how you still function in that role.

Don't search through the pages of your past looking for someone else to blame for your present problems. Instead try to understand why you are the way you are, so you can more easily change.

As you begin to uncover your codependent tendencies, there are two specific steps you can take to start dealing with them.

Let Go

One thing that makes overcoming codependent behavior so hard is feeling the need to hold on and control people in order for them to get better. Holding on seems like the safe thing to do.

Such isn't the case. Nobody will ever get better because you force them to. You can't rescue people who aren't ready to be rescued. The best thing you can do for them is to let them go and trust God to take care of them.

Consider again the story of the Prodigal Son, which we looked at in the last chapter. When the son wanted his inheritance, his father gave it to him. When the son wanted to leave, the father let him go. After he departed for the distant country, his father didn't search for him.

What would have happened if the father had followed his son to the distant land? He would have seen him wasting his life. Maybe the father would have stepped in and tried to reform him—like a hero. Maybe he would have tried to make things better by cracking a joke and saying, "Boys will be boys."

Intervention wouldn't have helped his son. The boy needed to reach a place of desperation. By letting go of his son, the father actually speeded up his recovery.

If you've focused your life on trying to rescue others, you need to let go of them. Continue to love them, but stop trying to control their behavior. Trust God to work in their lives.

Letting go doesn't mean you approve of wrong behavior. And it certainly doesn't mean you don't care. Instead you stop allowing yourself to try to fix others by controlling their lives.

You can show compassion and concern for friends and family members without rescuing them, without always feeling that it's your responsibility to bring things into balance, to make them better. When people share their problem with you, ask, "What do you need from me?" Once they've told you, decide whether or not you're able to help them. Set a limit on what you can do. If the timing isn't right for you to help them out, say, "I can't help you." Or it may be appropriate for you to simply listen and tell them you're sorry they're having problems. Offer your prayers and leave it at that.

After responding in this way, refuse to accept feelings of guilt and shame for not doing more. You did what you could, and that's enough.

Find the New You

Since your codependent behavior is rooted in your family of origin, part of the healing process involves recognizing that you don't need to function in those learned roles any longer.

I don't need to be a hero for my family or church. I don't have to make a joke to ease the tension in every situation. God didn't call me to rescue people who aren't ready to change. It's not my job to make everyone happy. And God didn't call you to rescue your parents, spouse, children, coworkers, or friends. In fact, as I understand the Bible, God didn't call us to rescue anyone. He does the rescuing. We are called to obey him and trust him to touch lives.

Overcoming our codependent roles involves more than understanding how our present behavior developed. Our inaccurate sense of identity is what drives us to rescue people. We feel safe and secure when we're needed. We feel righteous when we think we're helping deliver someone from their mess.

We need a new sense of identity, one that gives us security. A healthy identity begins with our relationship with God. In the next chapter you'll learn how to make him—not your lust or your need for human acceptance—your Master.

Thinking It Through

1. As you look at the diagram entitled "Profile of a Dysfunctional Family" in this chapter, which role best describes you? How do you find yourself acting out that role?

2. Which of the destructive actions of a codependent describe your behavior at times? Can you think of a recent incident in which you acted in one of these destructive ways?

3. Which of the negative emotions do you struggle with the most? How do you try to control it?

4. How does codependency affect a man's sexual compulsions?

5. What are the two steps to dealing with our codependent roles? How would you go about implementing those steps?

PART THREE

Finding Freedom

Chapter Seven

Choosing Your Master

I'm a barefoot water-skier. I love the exhilaration of skimming across glass-smooth water at high speeds. I love the spray of the water at my sides. And I love the challenge of performing tricks without skis.

Over the years numerous friends have asked, "Bill, could you teach me to ski barefoot?"

I always answer the same way: "If you're willing to repeatedly fall face-first while racing over the water at forty miles per hour, I can teach you."

Invariably they say, "I'll give it a try."

Once we're on the water, most of them give up after planting their face in the lake a few times. A few refuse to give up. They don't care how often they fall or how great the pain—they're determined to ski barefoot.

I've often contemplated the difference between those who persevere and those who give up. I don't think the issue is one of pain tolerance or courage or athletic ability. I'm convinced the difference is commitment. Some guys have made up their minds, before they step onto the water, that they'll ski barefoot, and eventually they do. Others like the idea of barefoot skiing, but unless it's easy, they'll give up.

When I teach someone to ski barefoot, I always try to make it clear up front how bad it hurts to eat the lake at high speeds. I encourage them to count the cost before trying it.

In a similar way, I want you to consider the cost of moral purity. If you've been hooked on pornography, prostitution, homosexuality, a romantic affair, or a host of other sexual sins, changing your lifestyle won't be easy. Even if you've not gone that far but find yourself thinking more and more about your sexual fantasies, returning to sexual purity won't be easy. Choosing to be pure means giving up something you enjoy. It means embracing discomfort and boredom. It means saying no to an intense craving for impure sexual pleasure.

Simply put, moral purity demands commitment. Before you make that commitment, I want to walk you through a process that will make it more meaningful—and hopefully, more permanent.

Count the Cost

In his book *Addictive Thinking,* Abraham Twersky observes that there's a law of human behavior that seems as inviolable as the law of gravity. He calls it the law of human gravity.

The law states, "A person gravitates from a condition that appears to be one of greater distress to a condition that appears to be one of lesser distress, and never in the reverse direction."[1] Simply put, Twersky contends that people choose the course of action that produces the least pain and the most pleasure.

When I first read Twersky's law of human gravity, I assumed it meant that the only people who break free of compulsions and addictions are those whose lives are in total disarray, those who have lost everything.

But that's not the way it is. Any man can find freedom from a sexual compulsion. But he will only do so if the pain of continuing in his addiction is greater than the pain of stopping. The pain of continuing can either be produced by losing everything he values or by experiencing less significant losses and contemplating the loss of everything.

My friends who learned to ski barefoot endured physical pain because they convinced themselves that the pain of failure was greater than the pain of falling. They endured the shock of slapping the water with their face at high speed because they could imagine the pleasure of success.

Yet once they had that vision of success, they still had to take a step of faith. They had to commit themselves and place one foot into the water and a moment later lift the other foot off the ski and put it into the water. They took that step knowing full well they were only a breath away from intense pain.

Nowadays ski instructors use a boom bar to help people learn to ski barefoot. A boom bar is a metal bar that extends over the side of a boat. The skier holds on to the bar, skims across the water on his backside, and when the boat reaches the right speed, he swings his feet around and skis barefoot. Boom bars diminish the frequency of falls, but nobody learns to ski barefoot without experiencing pain.

Similarly, there are things you can do to diminish the likelihood you'll fall back into sexual sins (we'll examine these in later chapters). But you'll never be pure without a willingness to undergo periods of discomfort. Since that's the case, you have to commit yourself to God and a process that will promote purity.

To help you make those commitments, I'd like to suggest you take some steps that will clarify your understanding of the consequences of sexual sins, the benefits of sexual purity, and the nature of devotion to God. The intent is to strengthen your willingness to make the kinds of commitments you must make to be pure.

Make a List

Most men don't have a tough time imagining the curves of a beautiful woman. We can mentally enjoy every feature of her face and body. But imagining the consequences of sexual sins isn't as easy. That's why it helps to actually write out a list so we can see them. With that in mind, take a few minutes and make a list of the consequences of continuing your harmful sexual behavior. Your list should include consequences you've already suffered. It should also describe the worst-case scenario if you don't stop. Use the list below and add to it if necessary.

Painful Consequences If I Continue

1. To my marriage:

2. To my family:

3. To my job:

4. To my health:

5. To my reputation:

6. To my self-image:

7. To my finances:

8. To my future:

Painful Consequences If I Stop

1. Boredom

2. Enduring emotional pain instead of deadening it with sex

3. Enduring an intense craving for destructive sexual experiences

4. _____

5. _____

Most men who struggle with compulsive sexual behavior reach a point of desperation in their life. This may be precipitated by a tragedy or crisis, such as the discovery of their secret life by their spouse or children. Or their compulsive behavior may threaten their job or health. Sometimes moving more deeply into sexual sins triggers feelings of intense guilt and shame. God can use these experiences as a wake-up call.

It may be the only way to get a man's attention is to hit him over the head with a two-by-four. If that's what it takes, God will do it. But there is a better way. That is to make a list and imagine the pain your sin will cause if you don't stop it. Hopefully, you'll see that the pain of continuing in your sin is greater than the pain of stopping. These lists are aimed at helping you say, "Enough is enough. I've had it. I want freedom, even if I have to endure pain to find it."

Once you've made these two lists, make a third one, which describes the benefits of moral purity.

Benefits of Purity

1. To my relationship with God:

2. To my wife:

3. To my children:

4. To my health:

5. To my reputation:

6. To my close friends:

7. To my self-image:

8. To my finances:

9. To my future:

Take some time to complete these lists. Use the suggested consequences and benefits as starting points. Add others that may apply to you.

As you examine these lists, it will become clear which choice brings the greatest benefits.

Unfortunately, when it comes to sexual sin, we men aren't always logical. We act like the man who was digging ditches during a hot summer day in Texas. After he had worked for several hours, a buddy said, "Why is it we're out here breaking our backs for minimum wage, while the president of the company makes a six-figure salary for practicing his putting in an air-conditioned office?"

"I'm going to find out," the man said, throwing down his shovel. He marched toward the office building that housed the company's executive suites. In a few minutes he was standing before the company president. "Why do you make so much money for doing hardly any work, while I dig ditches and make so little?"

The company president flashed a friendly smile and said, "Come over here, and I'll show you." He then held out his hand in front of a brick wall and said, "Hit my hand with your fist."

The worker hauled off and swung at the president's hand with all of his might. Just as his fist was about to make contact, the president moved his hand, and the ditchdigger's fist slammed into the wall. As he yelled in pain, the president said, "That's why I'm the president and you're a ditchdigger."

The worker returned to his buddy, who asked, "What did he tell you?"

"I'll show you," the worker said as he lifted his hand in front of his face. "Hit my hand as hard as you can."

It's hard to imagine anybody being that stupid. Yet we men can be just that illogical when it comes to lust. We'll do things that create unimaginable pain for ourselves and for those we love. I'm challenging you to resist the urge to be illogical. Look at the price of sexual sins and the benefits of purity and make a commitment to stop your destructive sexual behavior.

Turning away from sexual sins is the first commitment. The second involves turning to God. I don't think this is a two-step process. It's not as if we make one commitment and then the other. They occur simultaneously. When a trapeze artist is about to jump, he's making two commitments. He's committing to release the trapeze and to grab the catcher. Without both commitments he'll fall. The same is true of us. We must let go of our sin and turn to God.

Ending Isolation

Because lust is a spiritual problem, it isolates us from our inner self, from God, and from other people. The longer our lust runs unchecked, the more spiritually isolated we become. When lust is in full control of our life, we're unable to connect with God or others. Sin aims to smother our personalities and destroy our spiritual life. It wants to kill us.

In the early stages of an addiction, the object of our lust (the idol) seems to nurture life and bring fulfillment to our inner self. The rush of pornography or an affair exhilarates and makes a man feel alive. But as a sexual addiction progresses, the nurturing proves to be a mirage. That's why as lust consumes us, a spiritual withering occurs. For healing to take place, we must reconnect ourselves to God and cultivate our spiritual life.

Our willingness to grab hold of an idol in the form of a sexual object shows our need for God. It reveals the hunger in our soul for something outside ourselves. Saint Augustine wrote about this hunger centuries ago: "Our hearts were made for you, O Lord, and they are restless until they find their rest in you."

God wants to give you this rest. He wants you to experience union with him so you can grow spiritually. That's why Paul exhorts us to offer our bodies to God as living sacrifices (Rom. 12:1).

A Logical Choice

For a couple of years after I became a Christian, I struggled with the idea of dedication. The settings in which I saw people being exhorted to commit themselves to God were filled with emotion. After a moving sermon, people were urged to come forward and commit their lives to Christ. At youth camps, following a week of intense spiritual input, kids were exhorted to devote themselves to God.

Please don't misunderstand me. I don't have a problem with encouraging commitment at such times. God can and does use our emotions to draw us to himself. The problem is that when the emotions of the moment pass, the commitment sometimes goes with them.

I've had some intense religious experiences, and deeper commitment has flowed from some of them. But most of the long-lasting commitments I've made to God resulted from thinking through exactly what God wanted me to do and then deciding, by God's grace, to do it.

The apostle Paul had a similar approach to commitment. When he urged the Romans to present their bodies as living sacrifices to God, he said that such an act was a "reasonable" act of service (Rom. 12:1 NASB). In the original language, "reasonable" meant "based on logic."

Before asking them to make that commitment, Paul began his exhortation, "Therefore, I urge you, brothers, in view of God's mercy." The apostle used the word "therefore" because he wanted his readers to consider everything he had said to them in the previous eleven chapters. In those chapters he explained that God's mercy provides us with forgiveness, acceptance, freedom from lust, a wonderful future, and the power for a victorious life.

In light of all God has done for us through Christ, and in light of all he will do for us in Christ, doesn't it make sense that we should devote ourselves completely to him? Does pornography deserve our devotion? Does a prostitute? An illicit affair? Of course not! God alone deserves our devotion. And he alone can exercise his mercy on our lives in such a way that he prompts us to give ourselves to him in love.

Why Nots

I can think of several reasons why you may resist committing yourself to God.

You May Want to Wait Until You've Cleaned Up Your Act

Such thinking reveals a distorted understanding of God's love and power. God doesn't ask us to fix ourselves and then turn to him. He wants us to come to him broken so he can heal us.

God loves you just as you are. It's his power that will change you, not your own. Jesus compared our relationship with himself to that of a branch and vine (John 15:1–8). The job of the branch is to abide in the vine and bear fruit. It's the responsibility of the vine to produce the fruit. Similarly, living a sexually pure life is the fruit of a relationship with God, not the prerequisite.

The hymn that Billy Graham concludes his crusades with captures the essence of the message: "Just as I am without one plea, but that your blood was shed for me." A person becomes a Christian by simply trusting Christ to forgive his sins and give him eternal life. Christ died on a cross to pay the penalty for our sins and rose from the dead to assure us of eternal life.

The only thing left for us to do is trust in him. Our faith unleashes his infinite power to save.

As followers of Christ, we must commit ourselves to God and trust him to change us. Our faith taps into his unlimited strength (Eph. 1:15–23). That means you don't have to get your act together before devoting yourself to God.

You May Say, "I Committed Myself to God Before, and It Didn't Work"

I've heard that from scores of guys. Oftentimes they thought that when they committed themselves to God, the Lord would remove their lustful desires. When the lust remained, they concluded God had let them down. The truth is, God doesn't remove our lust—he gives us the guidelines and power we need to control it.

It Could Be You've Genuinely Committed Yourself to God in the Past and See No Need to Do It Again

Like wedding vows, our initial act of devotion to God occurs only once. But like wedding vows, that act can be renewed.

As a pastor, I occasionally have the privilege of performing wedding ceremonies for married couples who are renewing their vows. In some cases they do so to formally break with an incident of infidelity. They can't remarry each other, since they are already married. But they can renew their commitment to one another.

Sometimes men need to do that with God. They need to renew their act of commitment as a way to formally tell God—and themselves—that he is their Lord and Master.

You May Feel Unworthy to Commit Yourself to God

This objection involves feeling both unworthy of God's love and unable to change. If this describes your feelings, I want you to know you're right. You're *not* worthy of God's love, and you can't change yourself (Rom. 3:9–20; 7:23–24; James 2:10).

But guess what? Neither can anybody else. The Bible is filled with stories of men whose struggle with sin proved their unworthiness and humanity. Consider:

With Jacob it was deceit.

With Moses it was murder.

With Samson it was recurring lust.

With David it was lust and murder.

With Peter it was fear.

Don't kid yourself—even the most admired men in the Bible blew it. The Christian life isn't about being perfect and deserving God's favor. It's about taking a few steps, stumbling, getting back up, and taking a few more steps. Hopefully, over time we won't stumble as often or fall as hard. But one thing is sure: no matter how pure we may be, we'll never be deserving of God's favor. And we'll never be able to change ourselves. Since that's the case, we should devote ourselves to the One who loves us anyway and has the power to change us.

Give Yourself to God

If you'd like to dedicate yourself to God, I encourage you to do so now. Perhaps it would help for you to imagine yourself as a prodigal son returning to your Father. As you approach, you see him standing on the front porch of a great house. Right away you recognize him. The moment you've anticipated is here. To help deal with your nervousness, you rehearse what you'll say.

When you're about as close as a football field, he realizes it's you. Immediately your Father steps down from the porch and begins jogging toward you. As he gets closer, you can hear your heart beating. Suddenly he's there in front of you—smiling. Instantly he throws his arms around you.

Now it's time for you to tell your heavenly Father what you've done wrong. Express your sorrow. Tell him you're ready to commit your life to him. Let him know you're doing so because you want to serve him rather than your lust.

By doing this, you're placing your life in his hands. Unlike the animal sacrifices offered by the ancient Jews, you're presenting yourself to God as a *living* sacrifice. You're giving him your body for his use. Such an act is not only reasonable, it's deeply spiritual. You're to live your life for him and allow him to live his life through you. That's how you'll find the strength to control your lust.

A Crisis of Faith

Once you dedicate yourself to God, two things will happen. First, you'll be made aware of changes that must take place in your life. On August 21, 1971, Cindy and I stood before one another, exchanged vows, and said, "I do." Later we moved into a small apartment in Austin, Texas. It wasn't long before we realized we would both have to change if our marriage was going to work. I'd have to give up some sports and TV time for her. She would have to become more flexible.

A similar thing happens after we commit ourselves to Christ. God shows us areas of our lives that must change. While it's true that God accepts us just as we are, it's also true that he never leaves us that way. The Lord will show you thoughts and actions that must change if you're going to be sexually pure. He will point out things that can't be present in your life if you're going to draw near to him.

But a second thing will happen. As you contemplate these changes, you'll experience a crisis of faith. You'll be brought face to face with whether you truly believe in God or are merely enamored with the idea of faith in God.

During the time you've been indulging your lust, you've been trusting yourself to meet your needs for intimacy and pleasure. You've been relying on an object, a person, or an experience (and the demon behind it) to satisfy your longings. It will be painful to let go. Doing so will be like hitting the water face-first while traveling at forty miles per hour. It will hurt. Everything in you will plead to satisfy your lust once more.

At that point in time, you'll face a crisis of belief. Will you trust God to meet your needs or will you meet them yourself? Will you obey God or not?

There's no way around the crisis of faith. Throughout the Bible, whenever God called a man to himself, the man had to decide whether or not he believed God could be trusted to take care of him.

With Abraham, that meant leaving his homeland and traveling to an unknown country. He did that because he believed God would take care of him. Later he offered up Isaac as a sacrifice because he believed God would raise him from the dead (Heb. 11:17–19).

God has called you to dedicate yourself completely to him. By doing so, you're saying you believe God will protect you and provide for you. That act of commitment will bring about changes in the way you think and act. And it will lead to a moment in which you'll be forced to decide: "Can God meet my needs, or will I trust sex to meet them?"

Obviously, you're reading this book because you want to be pure. Many men dedicate themselves to God and then fall back into sin because they don't have a clear understanding of the changes God wants them to make so they can keep their lust under control. As a man who wants to be pure, you need to know the adaptations God wants from you. In the remainder of the book, we'll examine some biblical guidelines that God's Spirit will use to reshape the way you think and live.

You Can Do It!

In a sense, this process stirs up in me the emotions I experienced when I was into barefoot water-skiing. I feel the same anticipation I knew when a friend and I would get up at sunrise and drive to the lake. After arriving, we'd walk to the dock and climb into the boat. A two-foot layer of fog would hang over the surface of the glass-smooth water.

His dream was to ski barefoot. Mine was to help him. I had done all I could to prepare him for that day. He was ready and committed. I knew he could do it.

I know you can, too. And in the rest of this book, you'll learn how to build on your commitment to God, with a plan that will work.

Thinking It Through

1. Review the two lists of consequences for continuing or stopping your destructive sexual behavior. As you go over the lists, try to visualize the consequences of each decision. Ask God to enable you to be especially clear in seeing the consequences of continued sin.

2. Now review the list that states the benefits of purity. Ask God to help you see the blessings associated with living a sexually pure life.

3. Read over Romans 12:1–2. Are you at a place where you're ready to make Christ your Master? If not, why not? Ask God to help remove any barrier that's hindering your commitment to him.

If you've recommitted your life to Christ, tell a friend. It will help you and encourage them.

Chapter Eight

Discover the New You

One of my favorite episodes of *Star Trek—The Next Generation* began when the *Enterprise* encountered a strange probe, which emitted a beam that penetrated a very narrow region of the ship. Suddenly Captain Picard fainted. He found himself in the middle of a small village on the planet of Kataan, with a new name, Kamin, and a wife, Elain. It took Picard years to understand his new identity. Yet as time passed, he assumed the role of Kamin. He fathered two children, learned to play the flute, and tried unsuccessfully to devise a way to save the dying planet.

When Picard woke up on the bridge of the *Enterprise*, only twenty minutes had passed. And in that time he had lived an entire life with a new identity. Later Commander Riker handed him a small box they had found inside the probe. After Riker left, Picard opened the box and found his flute, which he cradled to his breast and then softly played. Picard realized he had become Kamin so he could pass on to others the story of a planet whose occupants had long ago died.

In a sense, that episode illustrates what happens to a man when he becomes a follower of Christ. After an encounter with Jesus Christ, his identity is changed. Initially he sees that things are different, but he's not sure exactly how. Over time he understands his new identity—he realizes he's a new man in Christ. Slowly Christ lives his life through the man.

Of course, the *Star Trek* illustration breaks down—as do all illustrations. But the point is this: when you trusted Christ, you became a new man, and it will take time for you to understand your new identity.

As I noted in the last chapter, once you devote yourself to Christ, God will point out to you ways you need to change. And no change is more important than how you see yourself. After we've dragged our shame into the light, confessed our sins, and devoted ourselves to Christ, we're ready to take the next step. Now we need to begin allowing God to change the way we view ourselves. In this chapter we'll begin that process.

Unconditional Acceptance

God's unconditional acceptance is tough to comprehend. You may wonder how he can overlook all the terrible things you've done. Actually, he doesn't overlook them. On the contrary—Jesus died on a cross to pay for all the wrong things you've done.

When I first heard this message, I was greatly relieved. While growing up, my family seldom attended church. And when we did go, I felt as out of place as a uniformed football player at a high-class concert. I saw myself as a sinner, and everyone else as a saint. I wondered what a person had to do to be right with God.

My religious friends gave me all sorts of answers. Some told me I had to go to church. Others said I had to stop swearing (fat chance, I thought) and be nice. Regardless of the formula, it seemed I had to win God's favor.

I realized that if the only way to please God was by being religious and toeing the line, I was in deep trouble. Real deep! I found church boring. I couldn't stop swearing. And I enjoyed chasing girls.

I was thrilled when I discovered that all God asked me to do was trust his Son to forgive me. God only wanted me to believe that Jesus paid for my sins through his death and offers me eternal life through his resurrection (Rom. 4:5; 10:9–10; Eph. 2:8–9). So one day I trusted Christ as my Savior.

What amazed me the most were the immediate changes that occurred in my life. Habits I had struggled with for years were shed like soiled and tattered garments. I was sure my lust and impure language were problems of the past.

Four Steps to Freedom

Of course, I was wrong. And when my lust stirred from its slumber after I had trusted Christ, it scared me. That's when I found, in the writings of Paul, some insights that altered how I handled my lustful appetites. The more I learned, the more I wanted to live free from the power of lust. When I began to experience what the Bible calls "walking in the light," I didn't want to return to my lustful appetites.

Step One: Know Who You Are in Christ

When Paul wrote his letter to the church in Rome, he knew some would say his message of salvation by faith promotes lawlessness. His critics would argue that if God freely forgives all who believe in Christ, nothing prevents people from satisfying their lower appetites.

Paul said such thinking fails to understand a spiritual reality. Namely, all who believe in Christ have been identified with him in his death, burial, and resurrection. This spiritual reality forms the basis of our new identity. Everything that's true of Christ (apart from his nontransferable divine attributes like omniscience, omnipresence, and omnipotence) is true of us. We're in Christ, like a page in a book. What's true of the book is true of the page.

As I mentioned earlier, Jesus compared our relationship with him to that of a branch in a vine. And when Jesus prayed on the night prior to his crucifixion, he said, "I pray also for those who will believe in me through their message, that all of them may be one, Father, just as you are in me and I am in you. May they also be in us" (John 17:20–21). While the Lord was talking about unity among believers, he was also recognizing our position in him.

Paul told the Galatians, "I have been crucified with Christ and I no longer live, but Christ lives in me" (Gal. 2:20). The old Paul, all he was before he met Christ, died on the cross. Now he was a new person—united with Jesus in his resurrection life.

In *Star Trek—Deep Space Nine,* Lieutenant Jadzia Dax is an attractive and brilliant young woman who looks like any other woman, except for a narrow banner of paisley-like markings that run across the side of her face and body. She's a member of the Trill, a unique race in which some people play host to another race that lives within them and is joined to them. Jadzia is the host to a three-hundred-year-old symbiot, Curzon Dax. Without losing her own identity or personality, Jadzia benefits from the experience and knowledge of Curzon Dax. The two are blended together in such a way that they are truly one.

In a sense, that's what happens when we become followers of Christ. The Spirit of the living God comes to dwell within us. In a mysterious way, God's Spirit intertwines with ours and we become a new person (2 Cor. 5:17).

Because we are actually new people, it would be inconsistent for us to live as we used to live. In Christ we have freedom from the power of sin and its lustful appetites (Rom. 6:1–14). Paul wrote, "We died to sin; how can we live in it any longer?" (Rom. 6:2). It's important to note that Paul didn't say that our sin, or lustful appetites, died. He said *we* died.

Since none of us has died physically, Paul had to be referring to another kind of death. He taught that all who believe in Christ are identified with him in his death, burial, and resurrection. It's not that we lose our individuality. Instead we are indwelt by Christ. Everything that's true of Christ is true of us.

This concept has life-changing power, because it describes a spiritual reality. It describes a new you.

Consider for a minute the implications of this truth. Does sin have power over Christ? Of course not! Since that's the case, it also has no power over you. Paul wants us to realize it's inconsistent for us to allow our lustful appetites to control our lives, since we've died and been raised with Christ. We're new people, identified with Christ. The risen Lord of the universe actually lives in us!

Several years ago I heard a story about a sailor who served under a harsh and demanding captain. After he had washed the deck, the captain would have him wash it again. After he had painted the railings, the captain would have him add another coat.

Finally the young sailor was discharged. No longer did he have to answer to the master who had controlled his every move.

Several weeks later the young man ran into his old captain on the streets of a harbor town. When the captain saw him, he gruffly ordered him to report back to the ship. The ex-sailor was so accustomed to obeying the captain's orders, he immediately turned toward the wharf. Then he remembered he had been released from the captain's authority. He no longer had to obey him or even listen to him. Instead of returning to the ship, he shook his head and walked away a free man.

The story illustrates what Paul is teaching us in Romans 6. You've been released from the power of your sinful lusts. Twice in the first six verses of that chapter, Paul uses the word "know." The first step in grasping your new identity involves knowledge. Like Captain Picard on planet Kataan, you have a new identity. You've been joined with Christ, and sin has no more power over you than it has over him.

Step Two: Believe You Live with Christ

Because you've been dominated by lust for so long, you may not feel as if its power has been broken. You may not feel like a new man in Christ. Regardless of how you feel, you need to know that Christ has shattered the power of sin in your life. You no longer have to give in to your lustful appetites.

Knowing that the power of sin has been broken pulls our foot out of lust's muddy grip. Believing we "will also live with him" (Rom. 6:8) enables us to move forward with our lives. It's our belief, our faith, in Christ that unleashes his unlimited power.

Jesus has called you to an intimate relationship with himself. All of his power and victory now belong to you. This truth is so real, Paul exhorts believers to "count yourselves dead to sin but alive to God in Christ Jesus" (Rom. 6:11).

You may not think you have enough faith. But you do. In fact, you exercise enough faith every day to unleash the power of Christ in your life. I suspect you have a car sitting in your garage, driveway, or carport. Under the hood of that car rests an engine. Almost every day you climb into the car, insert the key in the ignition, and start the engine.

That activity involves faith in the car, key, and motor. There may be days when the car is dirty and doesn't look as if it would go anywhere. On other occasions you may not feel like driving it anywhere. But regardless of how the car looks or how you feel, if the automobile is in operating order and you turn the ignition key, the engine will start. The car will take you where you want to go.

Christ's power over sin won't do you any good unless you utilize it. You do that by knowing that all that's true of him is true of you and by trusting him to live his life through you.

Step Three: Give Yourself to God

While you know how to start a car engine, you may be less sure how to utilize Christ's power. Paul gives us specific guidance when he tells us to give the members of our body to God as "instruments of righteousness" (Rom. 6:13).

The moment you're tempted to read pornography, surf the net for erotic images, flirt with a coworker, or visit a strip joint, you're making a decision based on how you view yourself. If you see yourself as a slave to sin, unable to say no to your sinful desires, you'll probably obey the commands of your master—lust.

If you see yourself as free from the power of sin, you'll present yourself as God's slave and walk away from the temptation.

How do you exercise faith in your car? You get in it, start the engine, and drive away. In other words, your faith is demonstrated by your actions. Similarly, you exercise faith in Christ by looking to him when you're tempted, and trusting him for the power you need to obey.

The next time your lust whispers in your ear, turn away from it and look to Christ. Don't struggle with your lust yourself. Don't resist it by saying, "I can't listen to it." Instead turn to God and say, "Father, thank you for delivering me from my lustful appetites. Thank you for giving me the power of Jesus. Right now I'm trusting in him to enable me to experience the victory he's given me."

If you try to fight against your lust in your own power, you'll lose. It's too powerful. Instead allow Christ to fight for you.

When I was in the ninth grade, Ron Kompton, a fellow student, despised me. Ron looked like a giant. He was a man among boys. He stood six feet three inches tall and weighed 230 pounds. I was only five feet nine inches tall and weighed 130 pounds. Ron's fist was almost as large as my head.

One night at a party Ron arrived late. When he discovered I was there, he hunted me down. In a few minutes he was calling me names and shoving me around. Like an idiot, I allowed him to coax me into the front yard, where he said he was going to kill me.

I did everything short of falling on my knees and crying like a baby to talk Ron out of beating me to a pulp—and I would have done that if I had thought it would save me.

We were standing in the yard surrounded by about thirty kids, who were urging us to get it on. Suddenly a car screeched to a halt at the curb. A moment later the door slammed and someone yelled, "Kompton!"

I recognized the voice. It was my best friend, Mike Temple. Mike was the only guy in town bigger and meaner than Ron Kompton. Before graduating from high school, Mike made the all-state football team twice as a fullback. Later he played college ball for Oklahoma State. He was a tough kid and loved to fight.

Mike quickly pushed his way through the crowd, walked up to Kompton, shoved him back, and said, "Kompton, if you're going to touch Perkins, you'll have to go through me!"

I felt a surge of courage and stepped up to Ron. "That's right, Kompton," I said. "And don't you ever forget it!"

Ron started whimpering about how he didn't realize Mike and I were buddies. He assured my friend he'd never bother me again.

I like that story, because it illustrates how Jesus fights for me. I don't need to suffer any more humiliating defeats.

By faith we believe that Christ has delivered us from sin and lust. Our union with him is the source of our self-control. We must believe that we're identified with him and that he is the source of our victory. We need to accept his victory in our minds and spirits.

Step Four: Don't Give Lust a Foothold

There's more to victory over sexual lust than knowing we're identified with Christ and have victory in him. The battle against lust isn't won by understanding alone. Nor is it assured because we have access to the power of Christ. We have to be diligent in our refusal to give lust a foothold in our life.

Paul wrote, "When you offer yourselves to someone to obey him as slaves, you are slaves of the one whom you obey—whether you are slaves to sin, which leads to death, or to obedience, which leads to righteousness" (Rom. 6:16).

It's easy to fall into the trap of thinking, "One little sin won't hurt. One look at an erotic image won't do any damage. One flirtatious conversation won't matter." Paul's message is clear: one sinful act leads to enslavement.

As you begin looking to Christ for victory over lust, your destructive appetites may hibernate for a while. You may think that an occasional experience with lust is acceptable, as long as you limit yourself. The thought may even occur to you that since God has forgiven you completely, an occasional sin won't hurt.

Paul's message is clear: "No way, José! One tiny sin leads to enslavement." Ultimately, you determine by your choices who will be your master. If you give your lust a small snack, it will demand your life. It will become your master. On the other hand, if you give yourself to Christ, he will be your Master.

Three Elements of Victory

Before we move on, I'd like to summarize what we've learned in this chapter. There are three important elements that will help the new you experience victory over sexual lust. It would be helpful for you to read these aloud until you've learned them. Once you have them memorized, frequently repeat them aloud.

Perspective

I'm a new person. I see my sexual lust differently. I'm united with Christ, and the power of my sinful nature has been broken. I don't have to obey its commands any longer.

The next time I'm using negative self-talk, in which I'm wallowing in my guilt and shame, I'm going to thank God he delivered me from that. I'm going to reflect on the fact that I'm in Christ and all that's true of him is true of me.

Presence

I'm not alone in my struggles. There is One beside me who knows my weakness and accepts me as I am—Jesus Christ, my Savior. The next time I feel alone, I'm going to remember that Christ is with me. Rather than looking to a sexual experience to meet my need for intimacy, I'm going to look to Christ.

Power

I have the power of the risen Christ living within me. I don't need to argue or fight with my lustful appetites. I don't need to vow to resist their enticements. When I'm tempted, I can turn to Christ and trust him to infuse me with his resurrection power.

Perspective, presence, and power are three elements that make up the new you. But living free requires another element. In the next chapter I'll give you a strategy aimed at helping you live free for the rest of your life.

Thinking It Through

1. When a man trusts Christ as his Savior, does that mean his lust problems are all behind him? Why or why not?

2. What kind of new identity did you receive when you became a follower of Christ? While you're still a sinner, why does sin no longer have power over you?

3. What steps can you take to enable yourself to experience victory over your lustful appetites?

4. Why is it so dangerous to give lust a foothold in your life? What kind of things do you do that might give lust a foothold? How can you prevent this from happening?

5. What are the three spiritual elements of victory over sexual lust? How can each one aid you?

Chapter Nine

Break the Addictive Cycle

Just about the time you think you're safe from an enemy attack—watch out. During the war in the Falkland Islands, the British Royal Navy felt that its ships were safe from attack, because of a sophisticated defense system that identified enemy missiles and shot them down. Attack after attack was repelled without any damage to a British ship.

And then the unexpected happened. The Royal Navy's 3,500-ton destroyer HMS *Sheffield* was sunk by a single missile fired from an Argentine fighter jet. Almost as soon as the destroyer hit the ocean floor, critics began to wonder if modern surface warships were obsolete sitting ducks for today's smart missiles.

A bigger surprise came when an investigation revealed that the *Sheffield*'s defenses did pick up the incoming missile. The ship's computer correctly identified it as a French-made Exocet. But the computer was programmed to ignore Exocets as friendly. The computer didn't recognize that the missile had been fired from an enemy plane. The ship was sunk by a missile it saw coming, a missile it could have destroyed.

Sometimes I feel that men who want to be sexually pure in our impure society are like great battleships floating on the open sea. Our downfall seems certain, because of the constant bombardment of sensual missiles that are fired our way every day. Our situation is only made worse by the fact that our defense system often allows these missiles to penetrate our mind—missiles we should see coming, missiles we could avoid.

I'm confident that you realize things have become worse in recent years. The proliferation of pornography has made it tougher to be pure today than it used to be.

A *U.S. News & World Report* cover story reported that according to *Adult Video News,* an industry trade publication, the number of hard-core video rentals rose from 75 million in 1985 to 490 million in 1992. The total climbed to 665 million in 1996. In that year Americans spent more than $8 billion on hard-core videos, peep shows, live sex acts, adult cable programming, sexual devices, computer porn, and sex magazines. That figure represents "an amount much larger than Hollywood's domestic box office receipts, and larger than all the revenues generated by rock and country music recordings."[1] If that surprises you, consider that Americans spend more money at strip clubs than at Broadway, off-Broadway, regional, and nonprofit theaters, and at the opera, the ballet, and jazz and classical performances—all together.[2]

Sociologist Charles Winick noted that the sexual content of American culture has changed more in two decades than it had in the previous two centuries. Just twenty-five years ago a federal study of pornography estimated that the total retail value of all the hard-core porn in the United States was between $5 million and $10 million.[3]

If you're a man living in the United States today, you cannot escape the impact of all this sexual stimulation. It's everywhere. What men used to have to drive across town to find in a sleazy theater is now offered in the privacy of the home. And all of this is done in an environment in which we're told it's healthy to indulge our sexual appetites—all of them, in any way.

Wouldn't it be great if you could commit yourself to God and immediately find yourself surrounded by an impenetrable force field, a defense system that would prevent any impure, sensual images from entering your mind?

Unfortunately, no such force field exists. Since that's the case, you need to develop a personal defense system that will protect your purity, a system that will enable you to identify and avoid the many dangerous situations offered by our sex-obsessed society. That's what I want to help you develop in this chapter. To do that, we'll examine the addictive cycle more closely and then devise a strategy for breaking it.

The Cycle According to James

We've already seen that we all have lustful appetites residing in our hearts. And make no mistake about it—your lustful appetites are obsessed with one thing: sexual gratification at any cost. When I was a kid, my dad once told me, "A hard dick has no conscience." He made a valid point. Once a man's lust is aroused, all sense of right and wrong goes down the drain. Men will sacrifice everything for a moment of sexual pleasure.

Our vows of commitment to God mean nothing to our lust. Why? Because a man controlled by his flesh (his sinful nature) is incapable of obeying God. Paul said as much when he wrote, "The sinful mind is hostile to God. It does not submit to God's law, nor can it do so. Those controlled by the sinful nature cannot please God" (Rom. 8:7–8).

In the last chapter we examined the new identity and nature that we have because we're in Christ (2 Cor. 5:17). We saw that as long as we're trusting Christ to live within us, the power of our sinful nature is broken. The problem is, a battle for domination is being waged within us. Our sinful, lustful appetites struggle against our new nature. Once we give our lustful appetites a beachhead, they'll take over our lives.

Preventing that from happening involves recognizing that our lust always assaults our mind in the same way. It repeatedly follows the same avenue of attack, because it's so effective. Fortunately for us, James, the half-brother of Jesus, has provided us with our Enemy's battle plan. Once we understand that plan, we can form a strategy for defeating it.

Earlier I noted the four stages of the addictive cycle — preoccupation, ritualization, acting out, and shame. Now we'll look at the addictive cycle through the eyes of James. The stages of temptation he mentions—enticement, conception, birth, and death—parallel those of the addictive cycle. While he wrote almost two thousand years ago, James clearly defined the cycle we struggle with today. He urged his readers to be aware of the cycle so they could avoid it.

Preoccupation / Enticement

James wrote, "Each one is tempted when, by his own evil desire, he is dragged away and enticed" (James 1:14). In the original language, the words for "dragged away" and

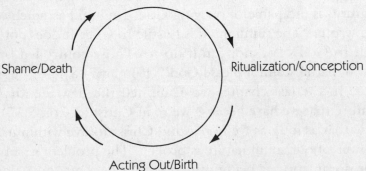

"enticed" are fishing terms. They speak of a fish being drawn out of its hiding place and attracted by a tempting lure.

Expert fishermen know where big fish swim and how to catch them. Mark, a friend of mine, is such a fisherman. He has spent years locating the best fishing spots in the Pacific Northwest.

Early one morning my oldest son, Ryan, and I climbed into Mark's Bronco. Mark was going to show us how to catch the big ones. After driving a few hours, we ended up by a river in the backwoods of Oregon. We hiked down a tree-lined trail to a rocky ledge overlooking a mountain stream.

"There are steelhead in there," Mark said, pointing to the deep, slow-moving water below us. "Bait your hooks the way I showed you and drop them in. You'll have a fish in no time."

Within a minute Ryan's rod bent down. His reel shrieked as a fish swam away with the hook. As Ryan pulled back on his rod, a three-foot steelhead arched out of the water. "Whoa, look at that!" he yelled. An hour later we had landed four fish. Ryan's weighed almost twenty pounds.

Mark's an expert fisherman who could earn a comfortable living as a fishing guide. He knows the right bait to drop in front of a fish to draw it out of hiding.

Unable to see the hook, a fish is captivated by the appeal of the bait. Even a granddaddy fish whose mouth is scarred from other hooks is vulnerable to the right lure.

How does a fish respond to temptation?

- He swims around the lure.

- He convinces himself there's no danger.

- He persuades himself he won't get caught.

- He tells himself he can take the bait and avoid the hook.

That's what happens to us in the first stage of the addictive cycle. Satan or one of his cohorts drops a sensual image in front of our eyes or in our ears. They may use an ad in a magazine or on a billboard, an enticing address on the Internet, a sensual scene on television, or a flirtatious coworker. Because these evil spirits have the power to enhance an object so it has a supernatural appeal, the object of our desire takes on an added beauty.

In a moment our lustful fallen nature whispers, "Looks good, doesn't it? It won't hurt to try it once. You'll enjoy it. You deserve it."

With little resistance, we listen to and believe the lies of our lust. We convince ourselves that we can play with the bait and not get hooked. We become blind to the danger of the hook and the hand holding the rod.

This is the stage of the cycle in which you must take aggressive action. You need to catch yourself daydreaming about pornography, affairs, strip clubs—or whatever else arouses your lust. If you find yourself fantasizing, switch mental gears.

When Satan tempted Jesus in the wilderness, the Lord didn't give the Devil's offers a second thought, even though the temptations addressed areas of intense need. For instance, Jesus hadn't eaten in forty days when Satan urged him to turn stones into bread. Jesus could have reasoned, "Why not? After all, hunger is a legitimate human need, and I have the power to make bread from stones." The Lord could have considered the suggestion of his enemy. But if you read the story in Matthew 4, you'll notice there is no gap between Satan's temptation and the Lord's reply. Jesus immediately quoted Scripture and rebuffed Satan's attack.

Such a response to temptation demands mental alertness. Peter urged us to "prepare your minds for action; be self-controlled; set your hope fully on the grace to be given you when Jesus Christ is revealed. As obedient children, do not conform to the evil desires you had when you lived in ignorance" (1 Peter 1:13–14).

Cutting off temptation at the enticement stage demands preparation, self-control, and a focus on Christ. How do we do that? In part by memorizing verses from the Bible. Like Jesus, we need to use Scripture to deal with temptation. I've found that memorizing large sections of the Bible gives me a safe mental focus when I'm tempted. By the time I recite a paragraph or two to myself, my spirit is strengthened and my mind is cleared.

The reason this works so well is because God uses the Bible to expose the danger of the bait. To the fish, a lure looks like the real thing. It gives the illusion of real food. Similarly, the object of our lust gives the illusion of intimacy. It promise us pleasure while filling the emptiness in our hearts. Meditating on the truth of Scripture helps us see the illusion for what it is. (In chapter 13 I provide you with some helpful verses.)

There's another reason why meditating on Scripture helps disrupt the cycle. Our minds can only think about one thing at a time. As long as you're mentally reviewing Bible verses, your mind is distracted from the tempting thought or action.

Of course, you may discover that your flesh is so aroused by the temptation that you don't want to resist it. Indeed, you want to fantasize about it. What you say to yourself at the moment of temptation is crucial if you're going to disengage your flesh and trust in Christ for his victory. As I noted in the last chapter, don't tell yourself, "I can't think about this. I won't think about this."

The moment you think like that, you're actually arousing your flesh. You're focusing on what you *shouldn't* think rather than what you *should* think. If someone told me to never visualize white elephants and I repeated to myself, "I won't think about white elephants, I won't think about white elephants," what am I doing? I'll tell you what I'm doing— I'm thinking about white elephants.

The more I do that with impure sexual images, the more I think about them and the more my flesh is aroused.

Instead I'm learning to tell myself at the moment I'm tempted, "Thank you, Lord, for saving me from that. Right now I'm looking to Jesus and trusting him to live his life through me. I'm now trusting him to use his Word to purify my mind."

Once I've said that prayer, I begin to meditate on Scripture.

If we don't cut off a temptation at the initial stage, it will progress to the next one.

Ritualization / Conception

After describing the enticement stage of the cycle, James changed imagery. No longer did he use the terminology of a fisherman. Instead he spoke of the birth process. He wrote, "After desire has conceived, it gives birth to sin" (James 1:15).

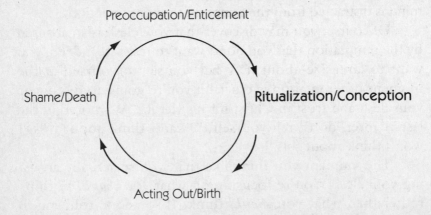

Preoccupation/Enticement

Shame/Death

Ritualization/Conception

Acting Out/Birth

At this stage we're beginning to give life to our thoughts. The seed of the act is present in our minds and growing. In fact, once the process reaches this stage, the act is virtually irreversible.

Like a pregnant woman buying baby clothes and nursery furniture, we anticipate an imminent delivery of the sinful act. While we haven't yet given birth to the deed, we're carrying out the rituals that precede it.

Nothing is more important for a man wanting to find freedom from sexual lust than identifying the rituals that precede an episode of acting out. Some of the rituals men have mentioned to me include

- surfing the Internet
- driving by a strip club
- reading personal ads
- browsing in a video store
- calling a former girlfriend
- television channel surfing
- cruising in a red-light district
- calling 900 numbers just for information
- asking a female acquaintance out to lunch

Each of us has unique rituals. Finding freedom means breaking the trance of those rituals. To do so, make a list of the rituals that lead up to your destructive sexual behavior. Once the list is made, define what you must do to contain the ritual.

Remember, abstinence demands that you stop performing your rituals. You must be willing to take any steps necessary to keep yourself away from them. Holding on to even one ritual will nurture your lust.

I know a man who removed cable television from his home. As a further precaution, he refused to watch television after 10:00 P.M. unless his wife was present. When I'm on the road, I refuse to turn on the television in my room. By never turning on the TV, I avoid the ritual of channel surfing. One man who used to sleep with prostitutes told me he takes an inconvenient route to work to keep from driving through a red-light district. (In chapter 13 I provide you with a chart on which you can write out your rituals.)

I've recently signed up with a new on-line server, Integrity Online, which blocks access to pornographic sites on the web.

These are examples of the kinds of aggressive steps that we must take to contain our lust.

As you make your list and prepare to break your rituals, expect your sinful nature to resist. Your sinful nature won't appear as a fire-breathing monster who's destroying your life. It'll seem as harmless as a kitten. Your lustful appetites will plead with you to keep one ritual—your favorite. It will promise never to ask for more. It will try to convince you that such actions aren't necessary.

You must anticipate the pleadings of your sinful nature and plan to ignore them. Make your list, and be ruthless. Identify every ritual that feeds your lust. If you don't, the next stage will inevitably occur.

Acting Out / Birth

Birth naturally follows conception. The act that has been dreamed about and planned will be carried out. The tantalizing bait will be tasted. If we don't break the cycle at the enticement or conception stages, it's unlikely we'll be able to prevent ourselves from acting out. It's as a friend of mine frequently says:

"Once you put your foot on the slippery slope, you're certain to fall." And once we fall, the outcome is truly painful.

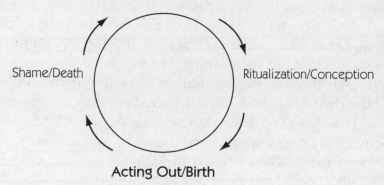

Preoccupation/Enticement

Shame/Death

Ritualization/Conception

Acting Out/Birth

Shame / Death

"Bill, I have a surprise," Cindy said. In a moment I would discover that she had a *big* surprise. "We're going to have a baby!" she exclaimed.

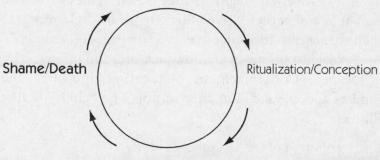

Preoccupation/Enticement

Shame/Death

Ritualization/Conception

Acting Out/Birth

I'll never forget the excitement of anticipating the birth of our first child. Cindy and I made a list of things we'd need: crib, drapes, rocker, diapers, changing table, night-light. What we didn't receive at baby showers, we found at garage sales.

We took a class in natural childbirth. I liked my role of standing at Cindy's side and reminding her to pant like a dog. Our doctor assured us that if she could focus on an object on the wall and concentrate on panting, it would diminish the pain.

They were right. When the big day arrived, I felt no pain at all. Cindy wasn't so lucky. At two in the morning on July 5, 1976, we raced to the hospital. We had hoped for a natural birth, but after four painful hours of labor, the doctor concluded the child would have to be delivered by cesarean section.

I was standing by the nurse's station when I heard the baby crying over a speaker attached to a microphone in the delivery room. Then I heard Cindy's voice: "Bill, God has given us a boy!" Later I joined Cindy in the delivery room and marveled at my son's tiny hands and feet. What a day!

Before Ryan was born, Cindy and I occasionally talked about the possibility of something going wrong. How horrible it would be if our son was stillborn after all those months of preparation and dreaming. I can't imagine a pain deeper and more lingering than that caused by the death of a child.

But death always happens after we sin. James wrote, "Sin, when it is full-grown, gives birth to death" (James 1:15). When we act out, the outcome is always pain and shame.

Sexual lust promises life, joy, pleasure, and intimacy. During the period of enticement, conception, and birth, these promises appear valid. But they're not. The "child" is always stillborn.

- Instead of life, lust gives death.

- Instead of joy, lust gives shame.

- Instead of pleasure, lust gives pain.

- Instead of intimacy, lust gives an illusion of intimacy.

Sinful sexual behavior always leads to despair. Ask King David. After his illicit affair with Bathsheba, he murdered her husband, Uriah. Later the child that resulted from the affair died.

Ask Samson. After his affair with Delilah, he lost his sight and sacrificed his place of leadership in Israel.

Ask the men whose names appear in the newspapers every week, men who have sacrificed their families and reputations because they didn't say no to their lust.

But go further. Have you ever acted out in a sexually sinful way and escaped the consequences? Perhaps for a while. But eventually you experienced loss. Nobody escapes the consequences of compulsive sexual behavior. Nobody! When we act out, we pay a high price.

But we don't have to sin. We can contain our lust and move forward with our life by breaking the cycle at its earliest stages.

Equipped to Help Others

It would be easy for you to wonder what good could come from your struggles with sexual lust. I understand how you feel. I look back on segments of my life with genuine regret. At times I wish I could erase them from my memory like segments of a videotape.

But I realize that my experiences—the struggles and failures—have deepened my dependence on God. They have helped me understand the suffering and struggles other men experience. Paul wrote, "Praise be to the God and Father of our Lord Jesus Christ, the Father of compassion and the God of all comfort, who comforts us in all our troubles, so that we can comfort those in any trouble with the comfort we ourselves have received from God" (2 Cor. 1:3–4).

I thank God that through his Son he accepts us as we are. He sees our failures and loves us anyway. But he does more. He wraps us in the blanket of his comfort and heals our hurts. Then he enables us to offer that same blanket of comfort and healing to others.

That truth brings us to an important place. As you find comfort in God and seek to break the addictive cycle, there is another step you must take. In fact, I'm convinced that without it, you won't be able to stand for long. You need to connect with other men. You need to offer them the comfort and encouragement of the Lord, and you need to let them support you as you seek to live a pure life. In the next chapter you'll discover how to do that.

Thinking It Through

1. How have the cultural values of our country changed in the last twenty years? How has this affected you?

2. According to James 1:14–15, what are the four stages of the addictive cycle? At which stages must temptation be resisted? Why?

3. What specific steps are you taking—or going to take—to resist temptation at those stages?

4. How can you use what you've learned to help other men maintain sexual purity?

PART FOUR

Living Free for the Rest
of Your Life

Chapter Ten

Why Locking Arms
Is Tough

If you've ever watched *Home Improvement,* you know that Tim Allen is a funny man. What you may not know is that he spent time in prison for selling drugs. How does he view his time behind bars? After reflecting on that question, he said, "Prison was the worst and the best thing that ever happened to me."[1]

In his best-selling book *Don't Stand Too Close to a Naked Man,* Allen tells about an experience he had while in jail. The event occurred right after he was placed in a holding cell with ten other guys. The first thing he noticed about the cell was that the toilet was in the middle of the room. He probably noticed that first because he had some business he needed to take care of. He said he looked at the can, then at the ceiling, then at the can, then at the ten guys in the cell. He wanted to leave. But the door was closed and locked.

He made up his mind that he would not use that can. No way! How could he take a dump with ten other guys watching? Finally, he wrote, "Digestion being as it is, things must emerge. I ambled tentatively to the can. I turned away and started back to my seat, but knew it was no good. I was committed. I sat down and suddenly all the men began moving toward me. I panicked.

"I didn't have to. This still blows my mind.

"What they did was form a horseshoe around me with their backs in my direction." Why had they done that? Allen said, "Because they're men, too. It was a big revelation. These aren't just losers like me, but they're *men*. They do this so you can have some privacy and no one can see in from the outside."[2]

That last statement is profound, because it describes what every man needs. We need friends who understand our fears and offer us protection, men who will stand guard around us during our times of vulnerability and shame.

It's too bad Allen had to go to jail to discover the willingness of men to shelter each other, to stand guard for each other. Because most men aren't forced into such close relationships, they never find that out. As I've talked with men, I've discovered most of them feel that their struggles with sexual lust are personal. They're private. They're shameful. Like a trip to the can—it's not the sort of thing they want other men to see.

Why Can't We Be Friends?

Because I'm convinced you need a few close friends who can understand your struggles and provide you with protection, we're going to take some time to understand why men resist open, intimate friendships with other men and how we can overcome this resistance.

"I Don't Have Time"

One reason most men don't have any close friends is because they don't have the time to build friendships. All of the guys I know are busy. Think of all the responsibilities they have to juggle: work, wife, children, church, household chores, recreation, community involvement, and other interests.

Each of those items I noted can require massive chunks of time. When a guy has a free moment, he wants to unwind.

He'd rather just recreate with other guys and keep the conversation at a superficial level. That way he can recharge emotionally, without the burden of any relational baggage.

Men like to spend their free time with other guys in "male zones." Those are the zones in which guys talk about things that interest men, things like tools, cars, sports, computers, technology, hunting, and fishing. Women like to connect at an emotional level. Men keep things on the surface. Conversations in a male zone don't run the risk of getting a man into something that will require more time than he wants to give.

The downside for men is that they have no one with whom they can share their inner self. And when a man reflects on the absence of close friends, he feels lonely. He remembers as a kid having buddies to whom he could tell everything. He told them about the problems with his parents and about the struggles at school.

But developing close friends takes time. Instant intimacy doesn't come in a box. Intimacy takes years or even decades to develop. It doesn't grow where the appointment book shields every relationship. While it includes entering into male zones and doing things like tracking deer, bait casting, fixing up an antique car, and coaching a kid's team, it also involves being there to listen and help pull a friend together when that friend's life is falling apart. It demands a willingness to let someone be there for us. An enduring friendship develops over years and grows through good and bad times. It involves hanging out together and sharing our innermost struggles, fears, disappointments, and victories. That kind of friendship demands something most men don't believe they have: time.

A pastor once asked a prominent member of his congregation, "Whenever I see you, you're always in a hurry. Your wife tells me you're always busy. Tell me, where are you running all the time?"

The man answered, "I'm running after success, fulfill-ment, and the reward for all my hard work."

The pastor responded, "That's a good answer if you assume that all those blessings are somewhere ahead of you, trying to elude you, and that if you run fast enough, you might catch up with them. But isn't it possible that those blessings are behind you, looking for you, and that the more you run, the harder you make it for them to find you?"

It seems to me, that's the lesson Jesus wanted Martha to learn. Martha was scurrying around the house, making prepa-rations for the Lord's visit. When he finally arrived, she just turned up the power and worked harder. Meanwhile Mary sat at the feet of Jesus.

Martha, disturbed by her sister's thoughtless behavior and the Lord's lack of concern, rebuked Jesus: "Lord, don't you care that my sister has left me to do the work by myself? Tell her to help me!" (Luke 10:40).

Jesus responded with words that apply to every obsessive-ly busy man: "You are worried and upset about many things, but only one thing is needed" (Luke 10:41–42).

With those words, Jesus underlined the importance of relationships. Martha had already prepared dinner. She didn't need to go to the trouble of fixing a five-course meal, especial-ly if her preparations reduced the time she could spend with Jesus. Her problem was, she didn't know when to slow down and focus on people. According to Jesus, Mary had chosen a better use of her time.

We've all heard it said that we make time for things that are important. It's true. And if purity is important, you'll have to make time in your life for other men—time to connect with them on a deeper level, time to help each other become all God wants you to be.

But even if you meet with a small group of guys, you'll still be reluctant to open up with them. One reason is because it's natural to see them as competitors instead of allies.

"I Want to Win!"

Bill Gates is the most famous businessman in the world—and the richest. It's estimated that his fortune is worth $23.9 billion. The 88 percent rise in Microsoft stock in 1996 meant he made on paper more than $10.9 billion, or about $30 million a day. But he's more than rich. Bill Gates is the Thomas Edison and Henry Ford of our age. (Since I wrote this, Gates' worth has increased to $39 billion.)[3]

You'd think someone with that much money and power could slow down. Yet Gates can't slow down, because he constantly worries about the competition. He once said, "In this business, by the time you realize you're in trouble, it's too late to save yourself. Unless you're running all the time, you're gone."[4] Rob Glaser, a former Microsoft executive who now runs the company that makes RealAudio, an Internet sound system, said of Gates, "He doesn't look for win-win situations with others, but for ways to make others lose. Success is defined as flattening the competition, not creating excellence."[5]

I've mentioned Gates because I think his obsession with beating the competition is characteristic of most men. Early in life boys discover the importance of winning. We're told, "A miss is as good as a mile." In other words, anyone who isn't a winner is a loser. During the 1996 Summer Olympics, Nike drove home this idea with a television commercial that said, "Silver medals aren't won; gold medals are lost!"

Of course, our parents and coaches always tried to soften the blow of losing. After a painful loss they would say, "You'll do better next time," "Nobody wins them all," "It's not whether you win or lose, it's how you play the game." But we knew that a first place always earned enthusiasm from our parents, friends, and coaches. And losing? It brought a gentle and somewhat sad expression of comfort.

As we grew, the words of our parents and coaches became our own. We developed our own inner voice that spoke kindly to us when we won and harshly when we lost.[6] Eventually we began to see other boys more as competitors than as friends. We viewed them as threats to our future success. Consequently we became more guarded around them. We learned how to hide our weaknesses to avoid giving other guys the upper hand. It's not that we're paranoid. We're not. We're just realistic. Or so we tell ourselves.

Even our closest friends don't really know us. They think of us as a pleasant man who is doing well with life. But all they see is the tip of the iceberg. They don't know the part of us that's driving, competitive, frightened, hurting, and lustful.

In a sense, our feelings were mirrored by the disciples. On one occasion the mother of James and John approached Jesus with her two sons and asked him to give them positions of influence in his kingdom (Matt. 20:20–21). Talk about guts! This mother wasn't lacking in nerve.

How do you think the rest of the disciples responded to her request? Were they excited for their friends? Hardly! Matthew noted, "When the ten heard about this, they were indignant with the two brothers" (Matt. 20:24). I suspect that one reason they were so mad was because they didn't think of that tactic for advancement themselves.

Like kids trying to impress a coach, Jesus' disciples struggled for recognition. What irritates me about the story is that I see myself in them. I try to hide my competitive spirit, but it's there.

Jesus dealt with the competitiveness of the disciples when he said, "Whoever wants to become great among you must be your servant, and whoever wants to be first must be your slave—just as the Son of Man did not come to be served, but to serve" (Matt. 20:26–28).

Jesus is asking us to make a paradigm shift. A paradigm shift occurs when we see things in a fresh and different way. Like the man who was driving his red Mustang convertible down a winding country road one spring afternoon. With the ragtop down, the man was enjoying the wind on his face and the wide open sky. Suddenly a woman in a late-model Cadillac came around a turn up ahead and almost ran him off the road. As she drove by, she shouted at him, "Pig!"

The man started to yell a name at her, when he rounded the turn and almost hit the pig standing in the middle of the road. In that instant he had a paradigm shift. He saw the world in a radically different way.

All our lives we've been programmed to win. Because of that, we see other men as competitors. Jesus wants us to change the way we view life. We're not here to compete with other men but to serve them. That doesn't mean all competition is wrong. It's fun to match our skills or those of our team against other men or teams. It's healthy to develop a competitive business or company. But for competition to remain healthy, it should be done with a spirit of love and compassion. Those we compete against are, after all, still men—just like us. We're not here to destroy them or to be greater than they are. We're here to help them become all they can be. We're to be their "wing man," their "blocking back," their "ringside coach."

As God's Spirit brings about this paradigm shift in our thinking, we'll still have to deal with another reason we resist getting close to guys.

"I Can Make It by Myself"

Even in a day when we know about the hazards of tobacco smoke, the Marlboro Man still carries a powerful image, especially for men. He's tough. He's handsome. He's independent. The Marlboro Man sits tall on his horse.

Most men want to be independent. That's why we don't like asking just anybody for instructions. We'd rather wander around for a while, unsure of our location or destination, than ask for help.

When we do ask for assistance, we only ask someone we're confident can help us. Women aren't that way. If I'm driving and Cindy thinks we're lost, she'll say, "Why don't you ask that guy standing on the street corner how to get there?"

One glance at the guy on the street corner tells me he's not a cop, a cabby, a firefighter, or anyone else who knows how to get around town any better than I do. At least, that's the way he looks to me. If I'm going to ask for help, I'm not going to ask just anybody. I'm going to ask an expert. Otherwise I'd rather solve the problem myself.

Because we guys like to solve our own problems, we're reluctant to share them with another man. After all, how can a friend help us?

Can you imagine the Marlboro Man riding up to another cowboy and saying, "I'm having a personal problem. Could I share it with you?" John Wayne never did that. Not once! Neither did James Bond. And neither will most men.

How do you think Jesus would respond to the philosophy of the rugged individual? I think he would point to a child and say, "Whoever humbles himself like this child is the greatest in the kingdom of heaven" (Matt. 18:4).

When I first read that verse, I wondered exactly how I was to become like a child. One thing is for sure: kids are self-serving. When they want something, they don't conceal their selfishness. I don't think Jesus meant that children are examples of sacrificial living. Rather he was pointing out that children live among adults as those who are helpless and weak. They are small people in a grownup world.

As men, we're to be like children. We're to act like the youngest in a large family. Why? Because that's the way we really are before God. We're like tiny, helpless, vulnerable children. And we need to see ourselves that way. But we also need to see other men that way. Only as we realize our weakness and need for close friends will we be willing to seek out such friends.

"I'd Rather Keep That to Myself"

I had just finished speaking at a men's rally when a slender, lean-muscled man wearing a polo shirt approached me. He was clearly upset about something and said he needed to talk. I told him if it was important, he might want to wait until the other men had cleared out. He nodded his head, refilled his Styrofoam cup with coffee, and sat in a front-row chair.

When the other men had left, I sat next to him and listened as he told me about the years he had struggled with pornography and masturbation. As a salesman, he was frequently on the road and found himself unable to resist watching erotic programming on television. What concerned him was that lately he had been visiting strip clubs. He wanted to know what he could do.

"Have you discussed this with any of your Christian friends?" I asked.

For a moment he was silent. He just stared into space. And then he looked at me and said, "No, I haven't. It's something I'd rather keep to myself."

"But you told me."

"Yeah, I did," he replied. "That's because you don't know me."

Most of us can identify with his feelings. We don't want to tell other men about our struggles with lust. As we saw in chapter 5, we're ashamed of the things we think and do in private. Yet as I noted in that chapter, it's crucial for you to tell God what you've done. Now you need to take another step. You need to tell a close friend.

Everything inside of you will resist doing this—your sense of independence, your competitive nature, your feelings of shame, your desire to fix it on your own, your lustful appetites. Like Adam in the garden, you'll want to run and hide. You'll want to keep doing what you've been doing—cover up.

If you want to be pure, you can't make it alone. You need other guys to offer you support. You need a few best friends to be there for you. Now that we understand why developing close friends is so tough for men, in the next chapter we're going to discover the stages of deep friendships and how they're cultivated.

Thinking It Through

1. What are the reasons men give for not developing close friendships with other men?

2. Which of those excuses have you used in the past? Do you think the excuses are legitimate? Why or why not?

3. What lesson do we learn from the Lord's experience with Martha and Mary in Luke 10:38–42?

4. In what way are we to become like little children? What would that look like in your life? How would it change your attitude toward other men?

5. Why is it so hard for men to share their struggles with other men?

6. Ask God to give you a willingness to develop close male friends. And then ask him to give you those friends.

Chapter Eleven

The Lost Art of Buddyship

"Show me the money, Jerry! Show me the monnnnnnnnney!"

While holding the phone to his ear, wide receiver Rod Tidwell sings those words to his agent in the movie *Jerry Maguire*.

If that statement captures the essence of big-time sports figures, Jerry's later confession, "I'm great at friendships but lousy at intimacy," captures the essence of the American man.

We're comfortable talking with men about inconsequential things, but we resist talking about our inner desires, struggles, and failures. Yet spiritual growth demands that men develop intimate friendships with other men. We need friends with whom we can share our darkest sins and greatest triumphs, friends who can help us stand when we're tempted and lift us up when we fall, friends whom we can provide with the same kind of support.

David and Jonathan had that kind of friendship. After the death of Jonathan, David lamented, "I grieve for you, Jonathan my brother; you were very dear to me. Your love for me was wonderful, more wonderful than that of women" (2 Sam. 1:26).

That astounding statement expresses a truth known by just about every man. Namely, there are aspects of male friendship that are unlike—and better—than what men experience with women. Men know such friendships are possible, but they don't know how to experience them. In this chapter, I want us to examine the phases of friendship and then find out how we can cultivate deep relationships with other men.

The Four Phases of Buddyship

I've often wondered how relationships pass from one level to the next. How do men become best friends? I'm thankful to Dr. Herb Goldberg for his insights. In his book *The Hazards of Being Male*, he identifies the four phases of buddyship (I've stuck with his phases but renamed the first two). Actually, the word "buddy" isn't one that men use much nowadays. Goldberg likes the term because it connotes youthfulness and spontaneity. He believes that this, when combined with adult maturity, contains the potential for the "ultimate in masculine friendship."[1]

The "Scratch My Back" Phase

Initially men connect with other men they believe can help them. It's an "I'll scratch your back if you'll scratch mine" kind of friendship. Because the benefits are high and the emotional cost low, most male relationships remain in this phase.

In the business world, such interaction enables men to help each other succeed. But the relationship is also expressed in other ways. It can assume the form of a teacher and student or a mentor and disciple. As long as both men benefit, the relationship will continue. When the mutual benefit ends, the relationship will fade.

Unfortunately, we've all seen back-scratching relationships that are harmful. That occurs when one man is used by another and receives nothing in return or when he's tossed aside like an empty can once his usefulness is exhausted. One of the painful lessons Jerry Maguire learns is that when he is no longer valuable to his company, not only does he lose his job, he loses most of the friendships he had at the company.

Several years ago I left a church I had pastored for nine years. Even though I've remained in the community, I haven't seen most of the men who were my friends. Why? Because I was connected to most of them by a common vision: to build a church. When we no longer shared a common goal, there was no need for our relationship. We're still cordial, but we no longer have a reason to connect.

I remember the surprise I felt when I discovered how superficial those relationships were. Fortunately, not all of my friendships were on that level. And neither are yours. Most men have a few friendships that go beyond the back-scratching phase.

The Recreational Phase

These friends are guys with whom we enter into the male zone. Our mutual interest in golf, racquetball, hunting, fishing, fixing up old cars, or coaching our kids throws us together on a regular basis. The activity provides the safe setting where we get together. Since the relationship revolves around the activity, there isn't a need for intimacy. In fact, if a man becomes ill, he probably won't see his friends or even hear from them until he returns to the activity. It's amazing that the members of a foursome can play golf for years and never really know each other.

The Friendship Phase

A relationship that reaches the recreational phase can develop into something more if both men have a natural affinity—that is, if they genuinely enjoy each other's company. When they talk, neither feels he must be right. When they play, neither has to win. They genuinely celebrate the successes of each other and like to talk about a variety of subjects.

Unlike the two previous phases, in this phase a man will offer aid to his friend and inquire if he's sick. He'll be willing to loan him money or a car. According to Jerry Seinfeld, a true friend will even drive you to the airport.

The Buddyship Phase

The deepest relationship between men is seldom reached, because it follows a crisis. Many of us remember as kids becoming closer buddies with a friend after a fistfight. Similarly, we become buddies with a man only after our friendship has survived a crisis that threatens to destroy the relationship.

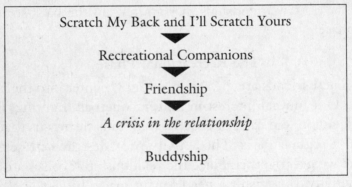

The breach is frequently created by an act of insensitivity that inflicts deep pain. It reveals the personal weaknesses and vulnerabilities that hadn't been seen before. Both men are wounded and face the temptation to abandon the relationship. In fact, that seems like the easiest thing to do.

At this point the friendship is teetering on the brink of destruction. The two men will either part and never be as close again or they'll work through the crisis and become buddies. Growth in the relationship occurs when they conclude that the friendship is more important than their wounds. It takes place when each sees the weaknesses in his friend and decides to remain friends.

Men who survive this crisis enter into a friendship that possesses deep trust. They know their buddy has seen them at their worst and accepts them anyway. It becomes a relationship in which at different times each serves as teacher, student, comforter, corrector, coach, and cheerleader. They now know they have a friend who will be there for them regardless of what happens.

Here's how Goldberg describes the relationship.

> There is a sense of warmth and empathic understanding and comfort when one person is feeling weak, acting foolish, or being vulnerable. In these instances one buddy gets stability and nourishment from the other. There is a happy, mutual sharing of resources, both material and emotional. The competitive element is inconsequential and a win for one becomes a win for both. The brother-brother dimension of buddyship is one in which each looks out for the other, protecting him from exploitation.[2]

Several years ago a close friend and I faced a crisis that threatened our friendship. After the death of his mother he went through a level of grief that devastated him. I had no idea he was hurting so bad. When he turned to me for support, I didn't give him the undivided attention he needed.

Hurt by my insensitivity, he told me to stay away. All of my attempts to reach out were rebuffed. Nothing in the history of our relationship had prepared me for this. He had always been an emotional rock. Previous problems had been weathered in a few days. But not this one. This one drove him to despair.

For over a year he kept me at arm's length. Throughout that time I determined that no matter how distant he tried to be, I wouldn't give up on our friendship.

One afternoon in his office, almost a year after the death of his mother, he said, "Bill, thanks for never giving up on me. I've been harsh with you, yet you hung in there with me."

For the first time in a year, he reached out to me. Amazingly, because neither of us gave up, we're closer friends than ever before. In the past he had seen my insensitivity but never suffered from it. I had seen his ability to distance himself from people but never felt it myself. Because of this crisis we saw each other's immaturity. Yet we hung in there. We weathered the crisis of our friendship and emerged as buddies.

Once a relationship reaches the phase of buddyship, it's fairly role free. Each man feels safe to act silly, stupid, serious, or even childlike. He can be himself without fear of rejection. He can openly share his failures and victories, because he knows he's unconditionally accepted.

The Art of Buddyship

Most guys remember what it was like to have a buddy when they were a kid. But as adults, men talk about their need for an accountability group to help them keep their promises to God and their wife. They perceive an accountability group as a place where they give an account for how things are going with their life. They don't think of it as a few buddies meeting because they love each other.

Since most groups begin at the "scratch my back" phase, this perception shouldn't surprise us. Men get together in accountability groups because it's mutually beneficial for everyone present. They aren't meeting because they like each other. They may not even know one another.

Initially a man will attend with the best of intentions. He intends to be open about his life. He intends to stop engaging in sexually impure practices. He intends to show up at all of the meetings.

But it's hard for him to meet with a group of guys he doesn't know very well. And openness isn't easy when he feels competitive with the other men. It's tough to lean on other men when he wants to demonstrate his independence. If he falls into sin, he'll want to skip the meeting altogether, because he wants to be seen as spiritual. Sadly, he may never return, because nobody will search him out.

Sometimes the members of the group will know something is wrong, but they're not sure what. In an effort to strengthen the relationships, they'll plan a fun activity to facilitate companionship—something like golfing, skiing, or fishing. That activity will help take the group to the recreational phase. But you need more than that.

You need a buddy or two. You need several close friends you feel safe around, friends who will be there for you no matter what you say or do, friends who will help you work through your struggles, friends you can coach and comfort.

It's those kinds of friendships in which accountability works, because you're meeting with men who care about each other. They check up on you because they love you—they want you to succeed. And you feel the same way about them.

In an instant society like ours, we expect such friendships to develop after a meeting or two. But remember, it takes time to move from the "scratch my back" phase of a relationship to the buddyship phase. What we need is an idea as to how we can facilitate the growth of a true friendship.

Commitment to God

Fortunately, God's Word offers us some help. In the relationship between Jonathan and David we find an example of how we can cultivate buddyship.

The first recorded instance of the two men meeting occurred after David killed Goliath. Jonathan was the son of

King Saul. He was a prince who, like David, had a daring faith in God. Before David's historic one-on-one battle with Goliath, Jonathan and his armor bearer had taken on and defeated twenty Philistines. Prior to the fight, Jonathan told his helper, "Nothing can hinder the LORD from saving, whether by many or by few" (1 Sam. 14:6).

The words of Jonathan were similar to those David yelled at Goliath when he said, "You come against me with sword and spear and javelin, but I come against you in the name of the LORD Almighty, the God of the armies of Israel, whom you have defied. This day the LORD will hand you over to me" (1 Sam. 17:45–46).

As men who want to be pure, we're involved in a spiritual struggle. Since that's the case, we need buddies whose faith will enable them to challenge us to godliness, confront us when we're wrong, and comfort us when we're discouraged.

When Jonathan heard the words of David and saw his heroic faith, he knew that was the man he wanted for a friend. And he determined to do all he could to cultivate the friendship.

The first thing you need to look for in a potential buddy is a devotion to Christ. He doesn't have to be perfect, and he won't be, but he needs to have a desire to grow in his relationship with Christ.

It's that commitment that prompts us to take steps to be pure. I mentioned earlier that after watching my neighbor talk on the phone, I confessed my voyeurism to my Saturday morning group. When two of them revealed they had been doing the same thing for over a year, I knew I had to take a bold step or I too would be hooked for years.

After the meeting I drove to my neighbor's house and told her husband (truthfully) that my dog had been barking lately at night. I also told him (truthfully) that a neighbor had reported to my wife that she had seen a man "peeking in her window one night." I let him know I didn't want anyone using my yard as a platform to invade his privacy and thought he should be sure to keep his shades closed at night.

He thanked me and said his wife had seen a man looking through their window one day, so he knew there was a Peeping Tom in the area.

That was a tough visit to make, and yet it immediately harnessed my lust. But it did more than that. It provided me with an opportunity to challenge my friends to take similar action—which they later did.

Ultimately, it was our passion for Christ that drove us to take those steps.

Commitment to Each Other

At some point in a relationship, you'll have to make a commitment to stick with your friend no matter what the cost. Jonathan did that with David. He made a covenant with him that was based on a mutual understanding and agreement (1 Sam. 18:1–4). They vowed to be true and loyal friends for the rest of their lives.

As a symbol of his commitment, Jonathan gave David a valuable gift. Because he was a prince, Jonathan was one of the few men in Israel with a sword. He gave David not only this but also his bow, belt, robe, and tunic. Jonathan gave David his most valuable possessions. In doing so, he was saying, "All I have is yours."

Talk about devotion! While you and I don't have a sword, bow, and belt, we do have something of great value we can give a buddy. It's something we talked about earlier: time. There is nothing you can give a buddy that is worth more than your time. I've found that I don't usually have to give it away in large chunks. But I do need to make weekly phone calls. I need to send E-mails to see how my buddies are doing. I need to be available if they want someone to talk with. I need to be willing to drop anything I'm doing for them.

One night I was facing a life-changing crisis that was brought on by events beyond my control. While I was talking with a buddy on the phone, he said, "I'll pick you up in the morning, and we'll spend the day together."

"But I thought you had to fly to San Diego to close that shopping center deal," I replied.

"I did. But not anymore," he said. "Now I need to be here for you."

That's the kind of support buddies give each other.

Jonathan did that for David in two ways. First, he ran interference for him. When Jonathan's father, King Saul, was trying to kill David, the young prince spoke with his father about David's innocence. Later he helped David escape the king's wrath (1 Sam. 19:1–7; 20:1–42).

Second, he encouraged David in the Lord. Exhausted by King Saul's relentless pursuit, the giant-killer despaired. Seeking refuge, David and his band of men hid in a cave in the desert hills of Ziph. Jonathan knew his friend was depressed. And he knew where he was hiding. Disregarding the wrath of his father, Jonathan found David and offered him hope. The prince told his friend, "Don't be afraid. . . . My father Saul will not lay a hand on you. You will be king over Israel, and I will be second to you. Even my father Saul knows this" (1 Sam. 23:17).

That brief encounter was the last time David would see his friend alive. But what an encounter! Jonathan reminded David that God would one day make him king. In saying that, Jonathan acknowledged that even though he was the king's son, it was David who would sit on the throne. Jonathan's devotion to David washed away any sense of competition or jealousy. Jonathan believed God's plan was for him to be number two. And if that was God's plan, it was good enough for him.

Maintaining moral purity is a daily battle. It's one that requires tremendous determination and teamwork. When I sense that one of my buddies is hiding in a cave, I go after him. When they sense I'm withdrawing, they come after me. Why? Because withdrawal is the first sign that a man is beginning to yield. At such times we need to follow Jonathan's example. We need to go after our buddies and strengthen them in the Lord. And we need to allow them to do that for us.

The question is, how can we do that in the area of sexual purity?

Connecting with a Purpose

Seven or eight years ago I was talking with a friend after lunch and asked, "How are you doing with the pornography when you're on the road?"

Taken aback by my directness, he smiled and looked away. "Why do you ask?"

"Because when I'm on the road, I find it an ever present temptation. I care about you and felt I should ask."

"I'm not doing well," he said. "But I want to."

The next week he joined two other guys and me for a weekly Tuesday morning meeting. Over the years we've come up with some guidelines and commitments aimed at helping us maintain purity.

1. My goal is to become like Jesus Christ. I want to keep the promises I make to God, to my wife, and to my children. I want to be sexually pure.

2. I'll always remember that each of us is equally messed up and vulnerable to sin.

3. I'll never discuss our specific struggles with *anyone* outside the group unless a crime has been committed or someone is in physical danger.

4. I'll never lie to a member of the group.

5. I'll always assume that everyone else in the group wants to hide their sin as much as I do mine. Because of that, I'm giving the other men permission to ask me specific questions about my behavior, questions that cannot be evaded. And they expect the same from me.

6. I'll identify the rituals that precede acting out and share them with the group so they can check up on how I'm doing.

With these guidelines in mind, begin looking for a friend with whom you can meet. Identify someone you think shares your devotion to Christ. Pick someone you sense wants to be pure. Ask if he's interested in meeting on a regular basis for mutual support and encouragement. During the first meeting let him know you're interested in cultivating a friendship that will help you keep your promises to God, to your wife, and to your children. Let him know you need the support of a friend to be pure and you thought he might feel the same way.

Be careful to move one step at a time. As you open up and share your struggles, give him time to feel safe so he can share his. As you talk about the temptations you face, remember that your goal isn't to support each other in failure. Your goal is to challenge each other to godliness.

As you discuss the guidelines I mentioned above, be sure to make it clear that neither of you is using them to control the other. Discuss them. Reword them. Make them your own. The sooner you do this, the better. Once you both accept them, you'll have permission to share more openly and probe more aggressively.

It may not take long for something to go wrong. One of you may sin and make excuses for missing the meeting. Something may be done or said that offends one of you. When that occurs, you'll probably ask, "What happened? Things were going so well."

Getting Past "What happened?"

When this occurs, God may be on the verge of moving your relationship from the friendship phase to the buddyship phase. Your tendency will be to give up on the relationship. But if you throw in the towel, your friendship will probably revert to a more superficial level.

Try to follow the example of Jesus and Peter after Peter denied the Lord. Jesus forgave Peter and assured him of his future usefulness. And what did Peter do? He accepted the Lord's forgiveness and learned from his mistake. In fact, he became more compassionate toward others. He urged us to "be sympathetic, love as brothers, be compassionate and humble" (1 Peter 3:8). Peter had learned firsthand about the value of those traits. And so must we.

If your friend falls into sin, he won't want to see you any more than you'll want to see him after you've stumbled. He'll resist telling you what he's done. He'll make all sorts of excuses for staying away from you. Your job is to hunt him down. Assure him of your acceptance and then ask him this question: "Have you done anything you shouldn't have since we last met?"

If he has, try to trace the source of his fall. Ask him which ritual got him back on the "slippery slope." Try to devise a strategy to avoid having that happen again. Remember, the key to purity is to cut off our lust at the preoccupation and ritualization stages. It's your job to help your buddy do that, and when he stumbles, it's your job to help him get back up again. His job is to do the same thing with you.

Don't Give Up

I recently asked the men in my Tuesday morning group, "How do you think you'd be doing if we weren't here for you?"

"I can't imagine that," one of them said.

"I know I'd have fallen into serious sin by now," another commented.

It's impossible for me to put into words how much I love those guys. I can't express how their comfort and confrontations have been used by God in my life. I want that for you. And I want you to know that it probably won't come easily. As I mentioned in the last chapter, men resist close friendships. You'll have to hang in there while that resistance is overcome. Relationships don't skip from the "scratch my back" phase to the buddyship phase in a few weeks. You'll have to persevere while the friendship grows. And in the process you'll probably be growled at and bitten by your friend.

I'm reminded of the story of the man who found a two-month-old black Labrador retriever lying in a puddle of mud under a bridge. It had a gash on its head, and its front legs were swollen where they had been bound with a rope.

The man approached the puppy to help it. When he was a few steps away from the dog, it stopped crying, showed its teeth, and growled. The man reached into his pocket and pulled out a strip of beef jerky. He squatted in front of the dog, talked to it softly, and tossed it a sliver of meat.

After several minutes he was petting the dog on the head and untying the tattered rope from its injured front legs. He then carried the dirty puppy home, nursed its wounds, and gave it food, water, and a soft bed.

The next morning when the man approached the dog, it snarled and snapped at him. Determined to befriend the animal, the man talked softly and gave it a piece of ham. Day after day he worked patiently with the black Lab. Finally, weeks later, as the man was watching TV the dog padded over to his chair and licked the back of his hand. The man looked down and saw the brown-eyed Lab looking up at him and wagging its tail.

I believe a lot of guys are like that dog. They've been wounded and bound by the world. They're suspicious of others and try to keep them at a safe distance. Our job is to demonstrate consistent love and kindness. If we want a buddy, we have to commit ourselves to a lifetime of loyalty and trust. We have to be willing to endure his growls and bites. But if we hang in there, one day we'll realize we have a close friend, someone who feels safe with us and with whom we feel safe, someone who helps us be morally pure while we help them do the same thing.

Of course, there is another relationship that is crucial if we're going to be pure, and that's the one we share with our wife. We'll discuss that relationship in the next chapter.

Thinking It Through

1. What are the four phases of male friendship? What characterizes each one?

2. What is the transition that moves a relationship from the friendship phase to the buddyship phase? Can you think of times when you had a friendship that didn't make it through the transition? Do you have relationships that did survive the transition? What was the outcome?

3. Why do men need male buddies?

4. How long does it take to become buddies? Why?

5. What can you do to cultivate closer friendships?

6. Review the guidelines for a group dedicated to helping members maintain purity. Which is the most important to you? Why?

Chapter Twelve

Pure Sex

One afternoon, a month after our wedding, Cindy and I were cleaning our apartment in Austin, Texas, when the phone rang. I picked up the receiver and was greeted by the friendly voice of a girl I had met a year before in Dallas.

"Hi!" she said. "I'm Diane. You met me at a party at Joe Glickman's house, and I told you I'd call if I ever came to Austin. Well, I'm here and was hoping we could go out."

"I'm flattered you called, but I'm married."

"Oh," she said, a bit surprised. "I guess that means you're not available any longer. Right?"

"Yeah, that's right. But thanks for calling."

After I hung up the phone, I was hit by the profound reality that for the rest of my life, I would never be able to date, kiss, hug, or express romantic affection in any way to a woman besides my wife.

"Who was that?" Cindy asked.

"A girl I met a while back who wanted a date."

Cindy smiled, wrapped her arms around me, and squeezed. "Well, you're out of circulation now."

That was twenty-five years ago. Since then we've faced the challenge of keeping the fires of romantic passion burning hot. It's easy for men to find sex boring after marriage. They can quickly tire of doing the same thing with the same person over and over again. When that happens, the appeal of pornography, an illicit affair, or a one-night stand becomes magnetic.

So far we've talked about how we can keep from acting out in sexually harmful ways. That's half the battle. The other half involves your relationship with your wife. In this chapter we'll consider some ideas that will restore passion to your marriage. If you're single, I hope these insights will give you something to look forward to when you marry.

God's Guidelines for Dynamic Sex

At first glance Paul's instructions concerning the sexual relationship between a husband and wife seem a bit superficial. But upon closer examination they provide four guidelines that can infuse significant sexual energy into a couple's marriage.

First: Your Body Belongs to Your Wife

Paul said, "The husband should fulfill his marital duty to his wife, and likewise the wife to her husband. The wife's body does not belong to her alone but also to her husband. In the same way, the husband's body does not belong to him alone but also to his wife" (1 Cor. 7:3–4).

You may read that passage and say, "Wait a minute. Paul is telling wives to regard their body as belonging to their husband." If you made that observation, you're right. Paul did say that. But those instructions were for your wife, not you. Her attitude is to be one in which she regards her body as belonging to you, her husband. But *she* is not to think that *your* body is there for her. And the opposite is true. You're to regard your body as belonging to her. But *you're* not to regard *her* body as being there for you. Each of you must remember that you're there for the other.

This is a crucial concept. It implies that your sexual energies are not for anyone else. They belong to your wife. Therefore they should be focused on her, not on another woman or on an image of a woman.

As we saw in chapter 1, it's normal for you to be sexually attracted to beautiful women. God wired you that way. But you must exercise discipline. The next time you see a woman and find yourself becoming aroused, stop and tell yourself, "I'm glad God created beautiful women and gave me the ability to enjoy them. But I belong to my wife." Instead of fantasizing about another woman, use the moment of sexual interest to refocus attention on your wife. Remind yourself that your body belongs to her.

Solomon urged us to do that when he wrote about a man's affection for his wife. He said, "A loving doe, a graceful deer—may her breasts satisfy you always, may you ever be captivated by her love" (Prov. 5:19). No matter how long a man has been married, he's to be intoxicated by the love of his wife. He is to always find pleasure with her.

Second: You're to Meet Your Wife's Sexual Needs

This reality flows logically from the previous one. If I'm here for my wife, it makes sense that it's my responsibility to meet her sexual needs. What's fascinating to me is that nothing turns on a man more than having his wife get turned on. We derive great pleasure from giving pleasure to our wives.

The problem is, most men forget that their wives are women. We tend to do for our wives what we want done for us. Of course, our wives do the same thing. If we're going to take Paul's admonition seriously, we need to discover what arouses our wives and do that for them. Since I can't possibly cover everything women like in one chapter, let's look at some of the most important things we can do to sexually stimulate our wives and in the process add some octane to the passion in our marriages.

Stay in First Gear!

My youngest son recently learned how to drive our five-speed Mazda Miata. I wasn't surprised that it took him a while to learn how to work the clutch. We can all remember that jerky experience we had when first learning how to coordinate releasing the clutch with pushing down the gas pedal.

What surprised me was how much trouble he had learning when to shift from one gear to another. Initially he would shift from first to second and then to third before he had enough RPMs to propel the car forward. We would find ourselves going up a hill without enough power to make it to the summit.

I think this driving analogy describes how men want to move from first to fifth gear with a woman before she has enough sexual energy built up to reach the summit. The reason we do that is because our sexual tachometer is hitting the redline after about five minutes, and we feel a need to shift gears.

One afternoon Cindy and I were involved in foreplay, and she was slowly caressing my shoulders, back, neck, head, arms, and hands. I thought to myself, "If I'd wanted a rubdown, I'd have gone to a masseuse."

Of course, she was doing to me what she wanted me to do to her. Since her engine was just hitting one thousand RPMs, she needed me to move slowly with her and not shift gears until she was closer to the redline.

If you want to meet your wife's sexual needs, stay in first gear until you sense *she's* ready for you to shift gears. Move slowly. Give her time to warm up.

It will help if you know what she likes. Don't assume she likes something just because you've done it a thousand times before. Ask her what arouses her. Find out at what pace and place she likes to be caressed. To help you do that, you might play a game Cindy and I engage in from time to time. I guarantee your wife will love it.

Select an evening when you won't be disturbed. Inform your wife in advance that you're going to make love to her according to her direction. Every touch and move will be at the pace and place of her selection. As your lovemaking progresses, remember: the goal isn't your gratification but hers. Find out how she likes her breasts, stomach, inner thighs, and clitoris caressed.

Follow Her Instructions

You'll probably discover that she likes you to remain in each gear far longer than you prefer. But do it. Slow down. Be especially open to instructions concerning how to stimulate her clitoris. Don't forget, this is the key to a woman's sexual gratification. A failure to stimulate her clitoris would give her as much pleasure as you'd get out of sex if your penis wasn't stroked. It's as if when God made the clitoris, he took all of the sensitive nerve endings in the penis, compressed them into a tiny point, and wrapped them in soft tissue. The clitoris is far more sensitive than the penis and must be handled with care. Even so, in most cases once a woman's clitoris is being stimulated, through intercourse or otherwise, it still takes longer for her to achieve an orgasm than it would take a man.

You'll likely discover that your wife won't want direct stimulation of her clitoris until she's wet. It's uncomfortable for the clitoris to be caressed when it's dry. Moisture around a woman's vagina is a sign of sexual arousal.

Amazingly, even Solomon made poetic reference to his bride's excitement and her secretion of fluid. He wrote, "You are a garden fountain, a well of flowing water streaming down from Lebanon" (Song 4:15). It's fascinating that under divine inspiration he praised the beauty and scent of his sexually aroused bride (Song 4:13–14).

As you become more proficient in sexually stimulating your wife, she'll become more aroused. As that happens, your own level of pleasure will increase. As I said earlier, nothing turns us men on more than sexually exciting our wives. But doing that requires discovering what turns them on.

Emotional Orgasms

One thing that may surprise you is that a woman doesn't have to achieve an orgasm every time in order to feel satisfied. When I was in seminary, the wives of seminary students met periodically to hear various speakers. On one occasion the microphone was made available for women to share brief testimonies.

After the meeting Cindy came home and could hardly wait to tell me what one of the wives had said. Cindy said this young woman had stepped up to the microphone and announced that what she would say would take a lot of pressure off some of the wives. The woman then said, "I always thought an orgasm was physical. Last night I had an emotional orgasm, and now I know they aren't physical but emotional."

Cindy and I both laughed, because we knew that someday that woman would probably have a big-time physical orgasm and be embarrassed about her announcement. But on second thought we realized she had made a good point. It's possible for women to derive real pleasure out of sex without having an orgasm every time.

As guys, we can't imagine that. Part of the reason is because for us sex provides a release of sexual energy. If we engage in foreplay and don't have an orgasm, it can actually be painful. On the other hand, for a woman tension builds up during sex. If the sexual tension doesn't build up to the point where she feels a need for an orgasm, don't pressure her into having one.

Crock-Pot Sex

Once you've discovered the pace and places that turn on your wife, try not to drive the same route every time you get together. As guys, we tend to get a technique down and repeat it over and over again. That's OK, but be sure to have several techniques you can use.

One of them is "Crock-Pot sex." That's the kind of sex that takes all day and night to cook. It begins in the morning with an extra-long hug and kiss as you leave, along with a promise to take her out to dinner. It's followed up with a phone call that communicates affection. Next comes a card or flower(s).

Notice I used the word "flower(s)." I did that because several years ago I discovered that every romantic act earns me one point with my wife. Both a single rose and a dozen roses are worth one point. Once I learned this, I decided to add up the points with more frequent and less expensive gifts.

Bring home a flower or a bunch of flowers. Put them in a vase and give her a kiss. I've learned over the years that Cindy loves to go for a walk with me. Find out if there is something special your wife enjoys doing with you, and treat her to that activity.

If you have kids, be sure you have a baby-sitter lined up for the evening. Remember, for your wife's sexual juices to heat up, she needs to be free of all pressure. During dinner tell her how much you love her, how much she means to you. If you're a less expressive man, tell her anyway. Even a casual reading of the Song of Songs reveals Solomon's frequent expressions of affection and appreciation for his bride. If you don't know what to say, here are some suggestions.

"You're beautiful."

"I'm glad I get to share my life with you."

"You have gorgeous eyes."

"I love to kiss your lips."

"Your kiss tastes sweet to me."

"I love to look at and caress your legs."

"I can't wait to touch you all over."

"I can't wait to feel your body against mine."

When you get home, take a bubble bath or shower together. After you've dried each other off, give her a massage and allow her to give you one. Once you get in bed, remember—go slow. Wait until her RPMs have approached the redline before shifting gears.

Crock-Pot sex isn't something you can do daily or weekly. But you should try it once a month.

Gourmet Sex

Because neither of us is a gourmet cook, we have to go somewhere else to enjoy such cooking. While Crock-Pot sex is great, it takes place at home. Occasionally you need to plan a getaway with your wife to a romantic spot. It doesn't have to be expensive. But it needs to be a place that makes her feel special.

For my wife's last birthday I surprised her with an overnight stay in an executive suite of a local hotel. Before we went out for dinner, I had her pack an overnight case. I bought a bunch of inexpensive flowers at a local grocery store (they still counted as one point) and had a friend take them to the hotel before we arrived. When Cindy entered the room, the flower arrangement was already in a vase sitting on a coffee table.

From that point on all I needed to do was go slow. The entire night was devoted to caring for her.

Microwave Sex

If you're willing to give your wife Crock-Pot sex and gourmet sex on a regular basis, she'll probably be willing to provide you with "microwave sex." In fact, it might be a dish she'd occasionally like herself. On those occasions when time is short, let her know you don't have time to fix a Crock-Pot but would sure like it if she would be willing to let you throw something in the microwave oven.

Of course, microwave sex comes in a variety of packages. They include intercourse, manual stimulation of the husband by the wife, or mutual manual stimulation. There are other kinds of microwave sex, and you and your wife need to feel free to do whatever turns you on, as long as it doesn't stimulate sinful lust or violate your conscience.

If this is the only meal on the menu, your wife won't be too excited about it. But if she knows you're committed to giving her what she needs, she'll enjoy taking care of your needs in this way.

Third: You're Not to Deny Your Wife

In his excellent book *Mars and Venus in the Bedroom,* John Gray observes, "Biologically and hormonally, men are much more driven to be sexual than women are. Quite naturally, it is on their minds more of the time. Because a man is wanting it so much, he will feel rejected more of the time when he is not getting it."[1]

The instinctive response when a man feels rejected is withdrawal. A man's spirit reminds me of the sea urchins that are found in tide pools on the Oregon coast. These beautiful creatures look like an open flower. But the moment a stick probes their soft center, the sea urchin will clamp shut.

Our wives can do a lot of things to communicate whether or not they are interested in sex. And we know how to read every signal. Do they face us or face away from us when they come to bed? Do they complain about how tired they are or talk about how affectionate they feel? Are they wearing sexy bedclothes or their old cotton nightgown? Do they tell us they have to get up early in the morning, or is sleep not an issue? Do they lock the door and put on romantic music before coming to bed or set the alarm clock? Once we begin to caress them, do they say, "That tickles," "My skin is sensitive tonight," "That doesn't feel good," or "Ouch!"

Because a man is so sensitive about sex, any lack of interest by his wife is like a stick in the spirit—it can shut a man down. And when that happens, a man will be hesitant to make any more advances. Over time he may lose interest in sex with his wife altogether.

We need to understand that the actions of our wife aren't usually intended as a sign of personal rejection. They may not even mean she doesn't want to have sex.

Sometimes when I ask Cindy if she's lovey, she'll say, "I don't know." When we first got married, I thought that meant, "No!" Later I discovered she meant she didn't know. Once I realized that, I followed her lack of interest with, "How about if we hug for a while?"

Guess what? More often than not she was in neutral and just needed me to patiently get her into first gear.

It may be that your sex drive is greater than your wife's. You may want sex three times a day, while twice a day is enough for her (just joking). But seriously, the differences in your appetite may cause you to frequently feel rejected. It's important to understand that your wife is probably not rejecting you. Her need simply isn't as great as yours. It's important to realize that God may have brought you together because he knew your wife needed the extra affection you could give her due to your additional sexual energy.

Regardless of why we feel rejected and hurt, we're not to sexually withdraw from our wives. To do so is sin. We're to take the time to meet their sexual needs, even when we feel like pulling away.

Fourth: Cultivate a Spiritual Connection

Paul said, "Do not deprive each other except by mutual consent and for a time, so that you may devote yourselves to prayer. Then come together again so that Satan will not tempt you because of your lack of self-control" (1 Cor. 7:5).

I've read scores of books about sex, and I've never once read anything about this particular verse. Yet I think it's critical for the sexual health of a husband and wife. Why? Because your physical relationship is intended by God to be a picture of your spiritual union. Nothing brings a couple closer to each other than prayer. Because God knows this, he says the only time you should abstain from sex is when you both agree to devote yourselves to prayer individually and as a couple.

The sad truth is that most men seldom pray with their wives. I'm not sure why. It may be because they feel spiritually inferior to their wives. Perhaps they don't think their prayers sound all that spiritual. Maybe they're just busy and don't think they have the time.

Whether or not you're in the habit of praying with your wife, I want to challenge you to try an experiment for one month. Every night before you go to sleep, pray with her. It doesn't have to be a long prayer, but make it real. In other words, don't recite a prayer you memorized as a child. Talk to God with your wife. Talk about the needs in your life, in your marriage, and in your family. If you haven't done this before, you'll be blown away by how close it brings the two of you.

Next set aside a time to abstain from sex so you can pray together. The period of abstinence needs to be related to how frequently you have sex. If you have sex every day, breaking for five days will be a significant time. If you have sex once a week, two weeks will be a challenge. Don't stop so long that you're tempted to satisfy yourself or look somewhere else for gratification.

This time of prayer will focus your life on the Lord, draw you together, and intensify your sexual appetite. It will cleanse you of any bitterness and renew your love. When you come back together again, you'll feel like newlyweds.

Enjoy God's Gift

For our twenty-fifth anniversary Cindy and I spent ten days in Hawaii. While we were there, we noticed scores of newly married couples. They were easy to spot, because of the way they held hands, walked arm in arm, and gazed into each other's eyes. We decided we would act like newlyweds during our entire trip. After all, the way we figured it, we were more in love than any of those couples could possibly be.

The more we expressed our affection physically, the more affectionate we felt. The more we expressed our love verbally, the more love we felt. I'm convinced there is nothing you can do to maintain sexual purity that's more important than loving your wife. Treat her as you did when you were dating, and you'll discover that some of the old fires are still there—they just needed to be stoked. Most men find that when the home fires are burning hot, the warmth of campfires isn't as appealing. Our job is to keep those home fires burning.

Thinking It Through

1. What are the four guidelines Paul gives in 1 Corinthians 7 for dynamic sex?

2. What are the three kinds of sex I've described? What are the things a man needs to do to meet his wife's sexual needs?

3. How can you discover what your wife enjoys?

4. What can you do to strengthen the spiritual side of your marriage relationship?

For additional insights on the physical side of marriage, I recommend John Gray's book *Mars and Venus in the Bedroom,* published by HarperCollins.

Chapter Thirteen

Tools for Tight Corners

Ernie Bellone, who lives across the street, has more tools he's never used than I have tools. No kidding. He says he likes to have them just in case he ever needs them.

It's amazing the difference a tool can make. Several years ago I snapped a fitting onto the end of a socket wrench to tackle a job I figured would take thirty minutes, tops. My plan was to take out the old kitchen faucet and put in a new one. Not a problem!

The job would have been easy, too, except my wrench wouldn't fit through the tiny space between the back of the sink and the wall. I tried every conceivable angle, but I couldn't get the end of the wrench over the head of the nut.

As you can imagine, it wasn't one of the most spiritual experiences of my life. Just as I was about to give up and do the unthinkable—call a plumber—I remembered Ernie.

After I explained my situation, he smiled. "I have a set of plumber's tools made exactly for that job." He pulled an unopened box from the top of a shelf in his garage and handed it to me. "It's a set of wrench extensions. You'll be the first to use them. I knew they'd come in handy one day!" he said with a smile.

Three minutes later I had the first nut off. Suddenly an impossible job became a breeze. The right tool solved the problem created by a tight corner.

Tools That Come In Handy

I hate to break the news to you, but as you move forward with your life of freedom from sexual lust, you'll occasionally find yourself in a tight corner. Try as you might, you won't be able to work your way out of it. Temptation, disappointment, or relapse will cause you to fear you're not going to make it. At such times you'll feel like throwing in the towel.

Instead turn to this chapter. Consider it a toolbox with all sorts of tools that will help you work your way out of tight corners. Read it carefully so you'll know where each tool is located. Mark those tools you may need first, so you'll be able to find them quickly. If you know the tools are here, someday you'll use them.

A Calendar

A calendar will serve you well. With this tool you can monitor your progress.

To abstain from sexual lust, you must live one day at a time. Don't think about quitting for a week, month, or year. Instead begin every day with a fresh commitment to avoid feeding your lust for twenty-four hours. At the end of each day mark your calendar to show another successful day completed.

If you relapse, indicate on your calendar exactly what triggered your fall. Over time you'll likely see a pattern of temptation emerging at particular times of the week, month, and year. You'll also begin to identify the kinds of situations that entice you.

Once you see the rhythms of your life recorded on your calendar, you'll be able to anticipate times of vulnerability and cope with them more effectively.

A Safety Guard against Rituals

A good power saw has a safety guard to protect your hands and allow you to cut wood without cutting off a finger. In overcoming compulsive sexual behavior, you need safety guards in place. It's crucial for you to identify the circumstances, conversations, and relationships that prompt you to act out. All trigger objects or events must have a safety guard around them.

You can construct such a shield by identifying the rituals that trigger your addictive behavior and removing them from your life. Use the following format to build a guard over your rituals.

Rituals	*How I'll Avoid Them*
1._____	1._____
2._____	2._____
3._____	3._____
4._____	4._____
5._____	5._____
6._____	6._____
7._____	7._____

Healthy Self-Talk

Since your lust wants to fill your mind with feelings of shame and self-hatred, you need to counteract its tactics with healthy, Scripture-based self-talk. Repeat the following phrase aloud throughout the day: "God unconditionally loves me, and I receive his love and accept myself."

The more you say it, the sooner you'll believe it. The sooner you believe it, the sooner you'll act like it's true.

A Support Team

If God intended for you to live alone, he would have put you on a private island. But he didn't. He intends for us to care for and support each other as we find freedom from our addictions.

Remember, true intimacy is an addiction's greatest enemy. As we saw in chapters 10 and 11, you need a friend who will love and accept you, pray for you, and speak the truth to you.

As you meet with your friend, the guidelines in chapter 11 are crucial. The first step in overcoming an addiction is admitting to God and a close friend that you're helpless. Once you admit that your life is out of control, it will begin to come under control.

But remember, your lust isn't dead. It will try to pull you into a mind-set of denial even after you've admitted your struggle with a friend or two. When you find yourself falling back into the trap, don't clam up. Whenever you deny your struggle, you're withdrawing from God and those who love you.

It's crucial that you speak openly with your support team about your struggles and failures. They need to understand your rituals and encourage you to avoid them. Honesty is the antidote for denial.

Patient Hope

Don't be surprised if after a few days or weeks of abstinence, your lust comes roaring out of its cave. Addictions are deep-rooted problems, and they take a long time to heal. The words of Isaiah offer encouragement: "Those who hope in the LORD will renew their strength. They will soar on wings like eagles; they will run and not grow weary, they will walk and not be faint" (Isa. 40:31).

Tools for Tight Corners   183

Pain

As you grow in your freedom from sexual lust, it's important to remember that pain isn't your enemy. Pain is a tool that will make you stronger. Don't run away from it or try to anesthetize it. Remember, you became addicted when you tried to anesthetize your pain. Eventually that which deadened the pain created more suffering than it eliminated.

Instead of running from the pain, ride it out as you would a rising tide. Eventually the craving to sinfully gratify your lust will recede.

Nobody passes through life without hardship. Even the apostle Paul experienced intense pain when he was afflicted with a thorn in the flesh (2 Cor. 12:7–9). While we don't know for sure the source of Paul's pain, we know he suffered greatly. Three times he begged God to take it away. Three times God refused. Instead of removing the cause of his suffering, God gave Paul an extra measure of his grace.

Rather than becoming angry with God, Paul wrote, "I will boast all the more gladly about my weaknesses, so that Christ's power may rest on me. That is why, for Christ's sake, I delight in weaknesses, in insults, in hardships, in persecutions, in difficulties. For when I am weak, then I am strong" (2 Cor. 12:9–10).

Paul learned how to rely on the grace of God during his times of suffering. While the pain wasn't removed, he experienced the strength needed to endure it with dignity.

Thankfully, that same grace is available to you. When you hurt, ask God to give you the grace you need to endure. Ask him to make his strength apparent through your weakness.

A Consequence and Benefits List

Usually the pleasure of acting out is limited to a few minutes or hours, but the consequences may last a lifetime. Many

men who were once addicted have found that comparing the
consequences of acting out with the benefits of abstinence
helps them avoid acting out. Periodically turn to chapter 7 and
complete or review the exercises outlined there under the
heading "Make a List."

Tears

Crying isn't something men do publicly. Some men
don't even cry in private. Yet tears are tools that help us heal. I
once read that tears are the body's way of washing away toxic
chemicals. Tears clean the body and soul. When we hold them
back, we dam up an emotional stream that needs to flow for
the heart to stay pure.

Even Jesus cried. When his friends Martha and Mary
wept over the death of their brother Lazarus, Jesus also wept
(John 11:35). His rough carpenter's hands wiped the tears
from his cheeks.

As you review the hurt you've suffered, you may need to
cry. Disappointment may have taken a toll. Go ahead and
weep. It's OK. Grieve over your disappointments and losses.
God understands. As you cry, imagine Jesus wrapping his
strong arms around you. God loves you and desires to heal
your hurts.

Forgiveness

Forgiveness is an invaluable tool for finding healing and
freedom from your lust. There are three dimensions of forgiveness you need to employ.

Finding forgiveness

No matter what you may have done, God offers you forgiveness. Regardless of how terrible your shame and torturous
your guilt, forgiveness is yours for the taking.

There is no need for you to continue to punish yourself for past wrongs. Jesus died on the cross and was punished in your place. He took upon himself all of your wrongdoing and suffered the punishment you deserved (2 Cor. 5:21; Rom. 5:8). Three days later he rose from the dead, leaving your guilt and shame forever buried.

His forgiveness is available. Simply express to him your desire to accept him and his forgiveness (John 3:16). Once you've been forgiven by God, there's no need to condemn yourself. When you hear voices of self-condemnation, say to yourself, "God forgives me and I forgive myself."

Extending Forgiveness

As God has forgiven you, so you must forgive those who hurt you. That's not easy, especially if your wounds are deep and festering. But healing requires cleaning them out by forgiving those who hurt you.

"But I can't forgive them," you might say. "You don't understand what they've done to me."

You're right, I don't. I'm sorry you've been hurt. But you've certainly not been brutalized more than Jesus was when the Romans nailed him to the cross. Yet God's Son extended forgiveness to those who killed him (Luke 23:34).

"But I'm not God's Son," you may argue.

I realize that. But if you'll turn to God, his Son will give you the strength you need to forgive.

There is a difference between forgiveness and reconciliation. Reconciliation can occur only when the offending person realizes the depth of hurt they've caused and seeks forgiveness. Even when reconciliation doesn't occur, you still need to forgive. You may forgive someone and never be reconciled with them.

Once you've told God you forgive the one who hurt you, each time you remember the hurt, pray for that person. Prayer is a great antidote for bitterness and wrath. In fact, I don't believe it's possible to harbor bitterness against someone you're consistently praying for.

Seeking Forgiveness

It may be you've hurt others while acting out sexually. As you reflect on your past, people you've hurt may come to mind. You may need to seek forgiveness from those people.

Before you get in touch with them, think through what you'll say. Avoid blaming them for your actions. Nobody wants to hear someone who's hurt them say something like, "After you lied and cheated me out of my money, I became angry and said some unkind words. Will you forgive me?"

Be honest and straight to the point. When I go to those I've hurt, I say something like this: "I now see that I've wronged you by (my offense). I'm deeply sorry. Will you forgive me?" I suggest you use a similar approach.

I encourage people to make these contacts in person or over the phone. Writing out your request for forgiveness isn't a good idea unless it's the only way to communicate with the person. A letter could fall into the wrong hands and cause greater pain.

Wounded persons are sometimes suspicious of attempts at reconciliation. They may even withhold forgiveness. Don't argue with them or try to persuade them. Tell them you understand, and request their prayers. If they pray for you, the time may come when they'll forgive you.

It's important to realize that people who forgive you aren't obligated to renew a relationship with you. You're not seeking total restoration of the relationship. You're simply seeking forgiveness. If something more occurs, that's great. But be careful not to place undue expectations on the other person.

Also, be sure to weigh the benefits of seeking forgiveness from a person you've wronged against the harm you could cause that person by approaching him or her about the offense. Sometimes the most loving thing to do is accept God's forgiveness and leave it at that.

Bible Meditation

Nothing helps me maintain sexual purity like memorizing and meditating on Bible verses that address my needs. Just as an addiction destroys the real you, meditation on Scripture nurtures the real you.

The following passages have proven helpful to me. Whenever I'm discouraged or tempted, I review them and gain direction and strength.

Temptation

"No temptation has seized you except what is common to man. And God is faithful; he will not let you be tempted beyond what you can bear. But when you are tempted, he will also provide a way out so that you can stand up under it" (1 Cor. 10:13).

"Blessed is the man who perseveres under trial, because when he has stood the test, he will receive the crown of life that God has promised to those who love him. When tempted, no one should say, 'God is tempting me.' For God cannot be tempted by evil, nor does he tempt anyone; but each one is tempted when, by his own evil desire, he is dragged away and enticed. Then, after desire has conceived, it gives birth to sin; and sin, when it is full-grown, gives birth to death" (James 1:12–15).

Anxiety

"Do not be anxious about anything, but in everything, by prayer and petition, with thanksgiving, present your requests to God. And the peace of God, which transcends all understanding, will guard your hearts and your minds in Christ Jesus" (Phil. 4:6–7).

Impure Thoughts

"Finally, brothers, whatever is true, whatever is noble, whatever is right, whatever is pure, whatever is lovely, whatever is admirable—if anything is excellent or praiseworthy—think about such things" (Phil. 4:8).

Lust

"Flee from sexual immorality. All other sins a man commits are outside his body, but he who sins sexually sins against his own body" (1 Cor. 6:18).

Contentment

"Keep your lives free from the love of money and be content with what you have, because God has said, 'Never will I leave you; never will I forsake you'" (Heb. 13:5).

Forgiveness

"Peter came to Jesus and asked, 'Lord, how many times shall I forgive my brother when he sins against me? Up to seven times?' Jesus answered, 'I tell you, not seven times, but seventy-seven times'" (Matt. 18:21–22).

"If we confess our sins, he is faithful and just and will forgive us our sins and purify us from all unrighteousness" (1 John 1:9).

"Blessed is he whose transgressions are forgiven, whose sins are covered" (Ps. 32:1).

Prayer

"The LORD is near to all who call on him, to all who call on him in truth" (Ps. 145:18).

"Ask and it will be given to you; seek and you will find; knock and the door will be opened to you. For everyone who asks receives; he who seeks finds; and to him who knocks, the door will be opened" (Matt. 7:7–8).

Self-Image

"Therefore, if anyone is in Christ, he is a new creation; the old has gone, the new has come!" (2 Cor. 5:17).

"For you created my inmost being; you knit me together in my mother's womb. I praise you because I am fearfully and wonderfully made; your works are wonderful, I know that full well" (Ps. 139:13–14).

"I have been crucified with Christ and I no longer live, but Christ lives in me. The life I live in the body, I live by faith in the Son of God, who loved me and gave himself for me" (Gal. 2:20).

"Since, then, you have been raised with Christ, set your hearts on things above, where Christ is seated at the right hand of God. Set your minds on things above, not on earthly things. For you died, and your life is now hidden with Christ in God" (Col. 3:1–3).

Prayer

Prayer is talking with God. It's the way you stay connected with the One who gives you his love and acceptance along with the power you need to control your lust. But your prayers don't obligate God to give you what you request. Just as a father sometimes says no to a child, so God may say no to you. His denial of a request doesn't show a lack of love. All of his actions are motivated by love.

If prayer isn't something you've ever scheduled, I encourage you to pray while you drive. Turn off your radio and carry on a conversation with God. Do it aloud. Once you develop the habit, try to carve out a time slot each day when you can get alone with God and pray.

Remember, the object of your lust gives you an illusion of intimacy. Only authentic intimacy with God will expose the illusion. Jesus made it clear that we remain in him through prayer and Bible meditation (John 15:7). God wants you to enjoy him so your need for the illusion of intimacy isn't there. View your times of prayer and Bible reading as opportunities to draw near to God.

Fasting

I mention fasting with hesitancy. Fasting isn't something done to lose weight or purge the body and spirit. It's a means of focusing the mind and spirit on God and nurturing your inner person.

Fasting softens my heart toward God and other people more than any other spiritual discipline (Isa. 58:3–1). It teaches me to say no to my appetite for food, which strengthens my will in other areas.

When you fast, try to take time for an extended period of Bible meditation and prayer. Ask the Lord to soften your heart and give you fresh direction.

If you're considering a fast, consult your physician about your plans. Make sure you get your doctor's approval and any suggestions your doctor may have.

Journaling

Each day I try to write in my journal. That doesn't mean I write pages of poetry. It involves recording the key events of the day and noting my spiritual temperature. I also try to write out a prayer or two so I'll have something to refer back to when my prayers are answered.

Keeping a journal is a tangible way of nurturing your spiritual nature. Remember, an addiction destroys your inner self. Bible meditation, prayer, fasting, and journaling strengthen your spirit by helping you develop intimacy with God.

Masturbation

While most men admit they masturbate at least occasionally, many are uncertain concerning the moral implications of the practice. The subject would be easier to deal with if the Bible provided a definitive statement on the subject. But it doesn't. As is often the case, when God doesn't address an issue, people develop differing views.

For instance, David Wilkerson, in his book *This Is Loving?* says, "Masturbation is not a gift of God for sex drives. Masturbation is not moral behavior and is not condoned in the Scriptures. . . . Masturbation is not harmless fun."[1] On the other hand, Charlie Shedd, a respected Christian authority on sex and dating, calls masturbation a "gift of God."[2]

Some who believe masturbation is wrong try to prove their point by referring to the Old Testament character Onan. After the death of Onan's brother, he had a responsibility to produce offspring with his brother's widow, Tamar (Gen. 38:8–10; Deut. 25:5–6). Apparently Onan wanted to have sex with Tamar but didn't want to father children. To keep her from getting pregnant, "whenever he lay with his brother's wife, he spilled his semen on the ground" (Gen. 38:9). Onan's behavior so displeased the Lord that he took Onan's life (Gen. 38:10).

Even a casual reading of this passage reveals that it has nothing to do with masturbation. God didn't condemn Onan for masturbating. He punished him for using Tamar to satisfy his sexual desire without fulfilling his responsibility to his brother.

When Is Masturbation Wrong?

It appears to me that masturbation is amoral. Under some circumstances it's acceptable behavior. On other occasions it's clearly wrong. As I've examined the Scriptures, I've observed three guidelines aimed at helping a person determine whether or not their behavior is sinful.

The Thought Test

In Matthew 5:28 Jesus said, "Anyone who looks at a woman lustfully has already committed adultery with her in his heart." While the act of masturbation may be amoral, fantasizing about having sex with someone other than your wife is clearly wrong. The words of Jesus would indicate that masturbation is wrong when accompanied by reading pornographic literature or viewing pornographic images. Again, the wrong isn't the act of masturbation but the accompanying thoughts.

The Self-Control Test

Masturbation that is obsessive is also wrong.

Several years ago a young man told me he masturbated four or five times a day. His entire life revolved around when and where he would masturbate. While his case is an extreme example, there are other men who find they can't resist the urge to masturbate. In 1 Corinthians 6:12, Paul wrote, "'Everything is permissible for me'—but not everything is beneficial. 'Everything is permissible for me'—but I will not be mastered by anything." While masturbation may not be wrong, it is wrong for our lives to be controlled by habitual or addictive masturbation.

The Love Test

During a counseling session a woman blurted out, "Bill, Shawn never wants to have sex with me anymore. When we first got married, that was all he wanted to do. Now we only have sex once a month, and that's when I beg him."

While meeting alone with me, Shawn told me, "It's just easier to read pornography and masturbate. I've done that for years. It saves me the hassle of dealing with my wife."

I wish I could say Shawn's behavior is unusual. It isn't. Men often prefer sexual gratification without intimacy and self-sacrifice. Obviously, when masturbation drains a person of sexual energy, their spouse will suffer the consequences.

In the last chapter we saw that the apostle Paul commanded husbands to meet their wife's sexual needs (1 Cor. 7:3). It's wrong for a man to masturbate when doing so prevents him from satisfying his wife's needs.

When Is Masturbation Acceptable?

There are as many unique situations as there are men. It would be impossible and foolish for me to try to walk though each one. I believe the three tests I've mentioned provide a guideline that could be applied to most situations.

Ask yourself:

1. "Does my behavior involve impure thoughts?"

2. "Am I in control of my behavior, or am I being controlled by my lust?"

3. "Is my behavior preventing me from meeting my wife's sexual needs?"

Ultimately, each of us has to determine before God whether our attitudes and actions are pleasing to him.

Relapse

I wish I could guarantee that you'll never relapse. I can't. But if you stumble, don't give up seeking freedom.

You may tend to think, "Now that I've blown it, I might as well quit trying." You must avoid such destructive thinking! If you relapse, rebound. You're not starting all over. Focus on the fact that you went for a while without acting out. Allow your disappointment to be a reminder of your vulnerability and need to depend on God. Let it be a reminder of the situations you need to avoid.

God has forgiven you. You must accept his forgiveness and move on. If the Lord of the universe has forgiven you, you don't need to wallow in self-condemnation.

A Final Thought

I wish the two of us could talk about how you can apply what you've learned. Of course, we can't. Books are like that.

But before we part, I want to remind you that nothing in life can replace intimacy with God, your wife, and a friend. Ultimately, a life of purity is a life connected with those we love the most, those who love us the most. Remember that. And remember that God is on your side.

Thinking It Through

1. Skim back through this chapter and mark the tools you think you'll need in the future.

2. Pick a Scripture verse that helps you the most and meditate on it for a week, asking God to help you experience the reality it represents. Try to memorize the passage.

3. Which of the ideas in this chapter will you implement first? Why?

Notes

Chapter One: *Why Naked Women Look So Good*

1. Tim Allen, *Don't Stand Too Close to a Naked Man* (New York: Hyperion, 1994), 53–54.

2. Mike Mason, *The Mystery of Marriage* (Portland, Ore.: Multnomah Press, 1985), 115.

3. Ibid., 114.

4. S. Craig Glickman, *A Song for Lovers* (Downers Grove, Ill.: InterVarsity Press, 1976), 21.

5. Ibid., 24–25.

Chapter Two: *Why Other Women Look Better*

1. Judson Poling and Bill Perkins, *The Journey* (Grand Rapids: Zondervan, 1996), 3.

Chapter Three: *I'm Caught and I Can't Get Loose*

1. H. Eist and A. Mandel, "Family Treatment of On-going Incest Behavior," *Family Process* (1967), 7:216.

Chapter Four: *Raise the White Flag*

1. Patrick Carnes, *Out of the Shadows* (Minneapolis: Comp-Care, 1983), 160.

2. Ibid., 27.

3. Craig Nakken, *The Addictive Personality* (New York: Harper & Row, 1988), 24.

4. Eugene H. Peterson, *The Message* (Colorado Springs: Nav-Press, 1993, 1994, 1995), 375.

Chapter Five: *Drag It into the Light*

1. John Bradshaw, *Healing the Shame That Binds You* (Health Communications), 12–13.

196   WHEN GOOD MEN ARE TEMPTED

2. M. Scott Peck, *People of the Lie* (New York: Simon & Schuster), 76.

3. Ibid., 76.

Chapter Six: *Your Family of Origin*

1. John Bradshaw, *Bradshaw on the Family* (Deerfield Beach, Ill.: Health Communications, 1988), 163–64.

2. Ibid., 165.

3. Claude M. Steiner, *Scripts People Live* (New York: Grove Press, 1974).

Chapter Seven: *Choosing Your Master*

1. Abraham Twersky, *Addictive Thinking* (San Francisco: Harper & Row, 1990), 79–80.

Chapter Nine: *Break the Addictive Cycle*

1. *U.S. News & World Report* (February 10, 1997), 43–44.

2. Ibid., 44.

3. Ibid.

Chapter Ten: *Why Locking Arms Is Tough*

1. Allen, *Don't Stand Too Close*, 84.

2. Ibid., 86–87.

3. "In Search of the Real Bill Gates," *Time* (January 13, 1997), 46.

4. "Billionaire Gates to Give Away Fortune in His Fifties," *Orlando Sentinel* (June 3, 1993).

5. "In Search of the Real Bill Gates," 56.

6. Herb Goldberg, *The Hazards of Being Male* (New York: New American Library, 1976), 115.

Chapter Eleven: *The Lost Art of Buddyship*

1. Goldberg, *The Hazards of Being Male*, 133.

2. Ibid., 136–37.

Chapter Twelve: *Pure Sex*

1. John Gray, *Mars and Venus in the Bedroom* (New York: HarperCollins, 1995), 86.

Chapter Thirteen: *Tools for Tight Corners*

1. David Wilkerson, *This Is Loving?* (Ventura, Calif.: Gospel Light, 1972), 40; as quoted by Jim Burns, *Radical Respect* (Eugene, Ore.: Harvest House, 1991), 158.

2. Charlie Shedd, *The Stork Is Dead* (Waco, Tex.: Word, 1968), 83; as quoted by Burns, *Radical Respect,* 159.

We want to hear from you. Please send your comments about this
book to us in care of the address below. Thank you.

ZondervanPublishingHouse
Grand Rapids, Michigan 49530
http://www.zondervan.com